"Dr. Rossella Valdrè's intr
topic of the death drive is c.

Among psychoanalysts th
cept, which has been remarka
has not convinced a significan
sion and has encountered outrig.

...at
...ic profes-
...other portion.

Freud came to hypothesise a   ...ctive drive driven by two
needs: to explain the failures of analytic work stalled by the tendency
of various patients to repeat the traumatic experience, their steely
determination to perpetuate their malaise; to make clear the human
destructiveness so dramatically manifested in World War I.

With his theorisation of the death drive, Freud laid the cornerstone
of his model of the homeostatic functioning of human mind-body matter: the tendency to return to a previous state of tension (to the constant
level of minimal tension – the constancy principle, or to the total absence of tension – the Nirvana principle). This model forms the basis
of every human being's defensive structure.

Criticism of Freud primarily concerns the difficulty of applying the
concept of the death drive in the clinical field without a certain degree
of schematisation. Repetition compulsion does not require a biological
foundation of its interpretive value. The same is true of the economic
discourse on masochism and in general the quantitative, defensive
functioning of the psyche that obeys the logic of need. Structural resistance to transformation in analysis is best explained by the rejection
of the feminine.

The death drive seems rooted, from the very French analysts who
most support its metapsychological importance, in the psychic impov-
erishment produced by its contraction that the destruction of the tie
with reality causes: the 'desire not to desire' (Aulagnier), the 'work
of the negative' that unties instead of tying representations together
(Green).

In her book Valdrè gives due importance to masochism. The link
made by Lacan between masochism/death drive and *malign* enjoyment
is well known: the pursuit of unlimited pleasure, the deadly, perpetual
hunger for pleasure. In the wake of his hypotheses, the idea of the
sexualisation of the death drive took hold in France.

Malign enjoyment has nothing to do with true enjoyment. Its presence stems from the dissolution of sexual difference that greatly hinders the unfurling and satisfaction of desire. Frustration creates tension
that must be discharged. Desire is thus perverted into need. A vicious

circle is created in which tension is produced and discharged. Because true fulfilment is not achieved, tension is recreated and is discharged again. Tension is constantly being produced, discharged, recreated, and discharged anew. The eclipse of desire and its perversion into need have a depressive effect. On the one hand, one desperately tries to keep alive desire perverted into need and on the other hand, one tries to feel alive instead of being alive and enjoying it, and remains in a loop of alternating between arousing and calming devices that mimic orgasm. Malign enjoyment is the fate of the frigid subject.

One might think that deadly masochism has its unconscious core in the identification with death, where sadism and masochism coincide, in wanting to be death, in the dual meaning of the omnipotent triumph over everything and the zero degree of tensions, the state of absolute Nirvana.

The death drive captures a condition of the human being, regardless of its roots in biology, which is more immediately tied to masochism than sadism. The psychic apparatus subjected to the 'work of the negative,' which operates through the reduction of the complexity of feeling, thinking, and being into patterns of mechanical, performative action, finds in the paranoid, aggressive setting not only a containment of depression (caused by the contraction of the relationship with reality) but also an effective way to discharge and defensively compact the organism. Destructive action is exquisitely self-destructive (destroying the other to destroy one's own suffering humanity) and sadistic excitement is inhabited at its core by masochistic excitement.

Valdrè approaches these difficult topics, so important for understanding human beings, with expertise, intelligence, and curiosity. Her book is very useful for any reader interested in psychoanalysis."

Sarantis Thanopulos, *President of the Italian Psychoanalytical Society and Training Analyst*

The Death Drive

This comprehensive yet accessible book analyses the clinical and historical experiences that led to the radical, complex and fundamental psychoanalytic concept of the death drive.

In *The Death Drive: A Contemporary Introduction,* Rossella Valdrè traces the path that led Sigmund Freud to theorise this key concept in his essay, *Beyond the Pleasure Principle.* She considers its roots in Freud's experiences of war trauma and his assessment of the human compulsion to repeat, as well as its consequences on his later theoretical and clinical work. Short vignettes from the clinician's room and examples from books and films introduce the reader to the birth and development of the concept, its biological and philosophical roots and its many clinical implications. Valdrè also reviews its varied reception among post-Freudians, and examines the controversies and questions that the death drive commonly engenders within the psychoanalytic community. She concludes by considering the death drive through the medium of art, its relationship with sublimation and the confirmation neuroscience is beginning to provide.

Written in a style that is at once accessible and precise, this book is an invaluable tool to students and psychoanalysts in training approaching the theory for the first time, as well as practising analysts, postgraduate students and scholars familiar with the concept and looking to explore it further.

Rossella Valdrè is a psychoanalyst, psychiatrist and Training Analyst of the Italian Psychoanalytical Society and International Psychoanalytical Association. She is the author of *Psychoanalytic Reflections on the Freudian Death Drive: In Theory, the Clinic, and Art* (2019), *Psychoanalytic Perspectives on Women and Power in Contemporary Fiction: Malice, the Victim and the Couple* (2017) and *On Sublimation: A Path to the Destiny of Desire, Theory, and Treatment* (2014).

Routledge Introductions to Contemporary
Psychoanalysis
Aner Govrin, Ph.D.
Series Editor
Yael Peri Herzovich, Ph.D.
Executive Editor
Itamar Ezer
Assistant Editor

"Routledge Introductions to Contemporary Psychoanalysis" is one of
the prominent psychoanalytic publishing ventures of our day. It will
comprise dozens of books that will serve as concise introductions dedicated to influential concepts, theories, leading figures, and techniques
in psychoanalysis covering every important aspect of psychoanalysis.

The length of each book is fixed at 40,000 words.

The series' books are designed to be easily accessible to provide
informative answers in various areas of psychoanalytic thought. Each
book will provide updated ideas on topics relevant to contemporary
psychoanalysis – from the unconscious and dreams, projective identification and eating disorders, through neuropsychoanalysis, colonialism,
and spiritual-sensitive psychoanalysis. Books will also be dedicated to
prominent figures in the field, such as Melanie Klein, Jaque Lacan,
Sandor Ferenczi, Otto Kernberg, and Michael Eigen.

Not serving solely as an introduction for beginners, the purpose
of the series is to offer compendiums of information on particular
topics within different psychoanalytic schools. We ask authors to review a topic but also address the readers with their own personal views
and contribution to the specific chosen field. Books will make intricate
ideas comprehensible without compromising their complexity.

We aim to make contemporary psychoanalysis more accessible to
both clinicians and the general educated public.

Erich Fromm: A Contemporary Introduction
Sandra Buechler

The Death Drive: A Contemporary Introduction
Rossella Valdrè

The Death Drive

A Contemporary Introduction

Rossella Valdrè

Routledge
Taylor & Francis Group

LONDON AND NEW YORK

Designed cover image: Michal Heiman, Asylum 1855–2020,
The Sleeper (video, psychoanalytic sofa and Plate 34),
exhibition view, Herzliya Museum of Contemporary Art, 2017

First published 2025
by Routledge
4 Park Square, Milton Park, Abingdon, Oxon OX14 4RN

and by Routledge
605 Third Avenue, New York, NY 10158

Routledge is an imprint of the Taylor & Francis Group, an informa business

British Library Cataloguing-in-Publication Data
A catalogue record for this book is available from the British Library

ISBN: 978-1-032-75587-8 (hbk)
ISBN: 978-1-032-68741-4 (pbk)
ISBN: 978-1-003-47467-8 (ebk)

DOI: 10.4324/9781003474678

Typeset in Times New Roman
by codeMantra

Contents

Foreword

This contribution by Rossella Valdrè, as quick and focused as it is precise, can be used as a small compass that points us to the meaning of Freudian metapsychology as a *reflection on human nature*.

Due to its fragility, humanity needs to be forged, shaped, by culture, just like a piece of pottery. We are not people, but *we become* a person, and we become a person in specific, culturally determined ways, cut and bent in different ways, on the intellectual, drive, emotional, ethical, and aesthetic levels. There is a plurality of forms of humanity, competing or competitive, even within the same context. Conflicts between humans are not only related to economics and power, but also to anthropological interests related to the various competing forms of humanity. We often forget that every forging produces offcuts, debris that streams forward and opens up the exploration of other forms of humanity; these are always constructions, partial and temporary, around our own helplessness. Through the dynamics of power, then, an attempt is made to impose a particular form of humanity, which purports to be just and natural (think of totalitarian regimes); then culture shows within its folds the *inhumanity* inherent to the human being, how it is tangled up with violence. Inhuman, in fact, alludes to the *not yet realised*, acerbic and emerging, but also to violence, prevarication, and the *undoing of humanity*.

It is precisely with respect to the "human-nonhuman" theme, which is at the centre of contemporary reflections, that this contribution by Valdrè is so valuable. It retraces Sigmund Freud's journey to imagining-understanding that the clamour of life does not only come from Eros, but also from the silent drives, from *death inside life*, as the introduction to Valdrè's 2019 book says. This mysterious *death* drive *is internal* to the individual, and, therefore, also to their history, but it is also at the heart of the dynamics of groups, institutions, and society as a whole. In this sense, as the author points out, the death drive should not be relegated to abstract and philosophical assumptions, but is reified in human life, both individual as well as group and social.

Valdrè shows us, through clinical glimpses and excursions into the art world as well, how the death drive is really a *desire to not desire,* a desire to return to that before life when we were not compelled to desire, when we could feel we were not in need of another human, and therefore we were limited and not omnipotent. When we could imagine ourselves feeling free even from the need to become a specific subject with their own thoughts and personal journey. David's retreat, F.'s self-punishment, Mark's story, Mrs. B.'s open book, the death drive in adolescents, the cinema of Lars von Trier, and poets and writers enliven this book with vital and fascinating testimonies.

The death drive is at the origin of isolated lives, *disinvestments,* the relationship, and the development of self that we often witness and that promise (illusorily) a sort of self-sufficient peace and quiet. On the contrary, they are the ones that trigger violence and destructiveness, in the inner world as well as in the relational and social world. Wars, like so many forms of individual pathology, emanate from a rejection of the human other, of need and of reality itself with the rocky limits it imposes on us.

We could say that destructiveness in an individual is an impulsion not to live, to let differences die, and to silence internal conflicts, but in this way, in fact, it becomes an impulsion to repeat, to never get well, as we see so often, and dramatically, in the clinic and in the daily news.

But Valdrè also highlights how the death drive is also necessary to life because it consists in the untying from objects, it allows the person to grow, to subjectivize.

Ultimately, in this contribution, Valdrè broadens the scope of a reflection necessary to the therapist, the psychoanalyst, the parent, and the teacher, steering it towards wider-ranging questions relating to what each of us understands by "human," thus avoiding any risk of settling on the obvious and the conventional.

In the book there is no shortage of clinical and theoretical references to the *primary traumatic elements* that support emerging disinvestment, isolation, and destructive violence. And Valdrè does so, drawing on many authors and psychoanalytic works, in a particular way: she takes us back to the child's need to encounter an *object they can hate,* an experience that allows the deadly drive to be extroverted and lets it meet Eros to modulate and transform it. Education, primary caregiving, today often seem, on the contrary, to demand from the child a total adherence, a seamless immersion in the family, or school, or group atmosphere, a conflict-free coexistence, showing impatience with the manifestations of the differences of the young, with their limitations and the specific sensitivities they communicate.

Lastly, Valdrè assimilates Freud's construction of the notion of the death drive to a *dream*. In these pages we thus find an implicit recognition of the relevance of the *method of psychoanalysis*, associative and fluctuating thought (like that of a dream), as a useful tool for each of us to approach the underlying questions around our humanity and our suffering. It is a stuttering, uncertain thought that goes from association to association, exploring, searching for some answer to the questions posed, without following a linear logic and without being regimented by it, without building within itself a hierarchy of thoughts. It is a complex thought that, while living, forms culture and forges the human through listening to the differences that the other, the child, the student, the patient, may bring.

Dr. Laura Ambrosiano
Training Analyst of the Italian Psychoanalytical Association

Acknowledgements

I am grateful to everyone who has helped me along the path to the publication of this book. To Routledge for inviting me to write about the death drive and to their editors for their support. My thanks also to my translators, Flora Capostagno and Kathryn Haralambous.

Introduction

Few concepts in psychoanalysis have caused such upset and confusion as Freud's death drive set out in his renowned 1920 essay *Beyond the Pleasure Principle*. From the outset, in fact, the psychoanalytic reception was divided between those who, in the footsteps of Freud, were and are in complete agreement; those who remained doubtful, above all on a theoretical level; and those who rejected it, starting with upholders of the theory of objective relations to those of modern intersubjectivity. This book, which the new series *A Contemporary Introduction in Psychoanalysis* quite rightly includes, intends to clarify the history and spirit of this fundamental Freudian concept, which, in my opinion, should not be limited to those who remain loyal to Freud, but is fundamental in psychoanalysis itself and even in reflections on human nature. It must be said that today in contemporary psychoanalysis, which has been able to accept so many different natures, the concept of the death drive arouses less asperity and is substantially accepted on a clinical level because, as we will see, parts of the post-Kleinian environments have approached it (with the very similar Nirvana-like concept)[1] and it has piqued interest in the field of neuroscience.

If we ask ourselves why the Freudian death drive has caused so much confusion and division, I believe we can venture the hypothesis that *Beyond the Pleasure Principle* is an innovative, thorny, and indefinable piece of writing. Freud himself called it "speculation, often far-fetched speculation" (Freud, 1920, p. 210). A creative effort of his imagination, it tries to combine the psychic and the biological, and a vision of the human being that gives reason to numerous clinical facts that do not respond to the principle of pleasure.

DOI: 10.4324/9781003474678-1

I agree with Jean Laplanche that we need to distinguish speculation and theory. Both can be considered defensive, while this speculation is comparable in a certain way to a work of art, insensitive to contradiction, and this is precisely the mark of the transition to the unconscious so that, faced with these contradictions, we must at the same time interpret and respect them and avoid flattening them (2008). Therefore, speculation here is to be understood as something that dares hypothesis, is not really theoretical or clinical, and almost resembles a dream. Yet we cannot fail to recognize that psychoanalysis, in order to advance on its path, also needs great speculations that eventually are more or less confirmed.

The death drive, that, as we will see, will be theorized by Freud on the observation of some inexplicable clinical facts and on the observation of war trauma, could be defined as the push, *internal to the human being*, to reset tensions and excitement, to return to a "before" of life, to restore quiet and homeostasis. However, as long as there is life in the organism it does not work alone but combines, continuously mixes with Eros, the life drive: we stay alive inasmuch as the two drives of life and death live together and fight together, for neither only with Eros nor, of course, only with Thanatos is life possible. Death, then, is within life.

In this book I will retrace the birth and development of the concept in Freudian thought, which, although fully theorized in 1920, was in Freud's mind even as far back as *Project for a Scientific Psychology* in 1895. The idea of a "principle of constancy" or "inertia" which regulates the psychic apparatus was already present, never abandoned. I will then continue with metapsychological insights into this strange drive, which some people do not think can even strictly be called a drive, in particular Francophone authors who are the most faithful heirs of Freudian thought. I will then go on to the death drive in post-Freudian thought and, in particular, the persisting confusion surrounding the much easier concept of aggression.

Another important chapter concerns the so-called derivatives of the death drive: how it expresses itself clinically. Where and how do we find it, given that Freud defines the death drive as "mute" with respect to the great clamour that Eros brings in life? After observing the clinical facts that led him to this theory of repetition, traumatic dreams, negative therapeutic reactions, Freud faces another fundamental expression of the "beyond" of pleasure, namely masochism. I will use vignettes from my clinical practice to discuss the key subject of masochism, the death drive's main derivative, as well as negative therapeutic reaction and some forms of repetition and psychopathologies, such as melancholy.

The importance of masochism is decisive as an often-silent expression of the death drive, so much so that Freud devotes an essay to it four years later, in 1924, *The Economic Problem of Masochism*. The mystery of masochism in human life, its "enigma," as Freud defines it, is far from being solved. The interest of the death drive, a concept that, as mentioned, affects human nature, is not limited to the individual but, as a drive *internal* to the individual, it can be equally active in groups, institutions, and society as a whole. I will conclude this reflection with some thoughts regarding the artistic sphere and current developments in neuroscience: while artists, as Freud has always said, know everything first thanks to their intuition and have given us many expressions of the death drive, human sciences are slower to get there.

There is not much literature on the death drive for the English-speaking reader, even if we have recently seen a resurgence of interest. The reasons for this interest, in my opinion, are not so much related to possible neuroscientific confirmation, but to the observation, as Freud said in his letter to Einstein in 1932, of how deep self-destruction is in a person, the urge not to live and, often in our patients, not to heal. The Freudian death drive offers us one of the best, if not the only, hypothesis able to explain in psychoanalytic terms this paradoxical thrust of the human being.

Note

1 I recall the concept of "common ground" introduced by Wallerstein at the end of the 1980s, regarding coexistence in contemporary psychoanalysis of different orientations. Wallerstein R.S. (1990): Psychoanalysis: The common ground. *International Journal of Psychoanalysis*, 71: 3–20.

Chapter 1

The death drive in Freudian thought

Theory and historical context

Historical context

> (...) but I can no longer understand how we have overlooked the
> ubiquity of non-erotic aggressivity and destructiveness and can
> have failed to give it its due place in our interpretation of life (...).
> I remember my own defensive attitude when the idea of an instinct
> of destruction first emerged in psycho-analytic literature, *and how
> long it took me before I became receptive to it.*
>
> (Freud, 1929, p. 99, my italics)

When, towards the end of his thoughts, he writes bitter words about
human nature in *Civilization and Its Discontents* (1929), to Freud it
seems strange to have taken so long to theorize a death drive whose
existence is now evident. But how does he actually get there?

We must place, as always in Freudian thought, the theorization of
the death drive within the historical context of its birth in his 1920 essay *Beyond the Pleasure Principle.*[1] The Great War has just ended. It
makes a huge impact on the world, and Freud is no exception. Europe
is a devastated continent, and psychoanalysis is confronted with a new
type of patient, the traumatized war veteran, whose numbers are great
and who presents a surprising clinical phenomenon, the often very
painful repetition of dreams that instead of representing any realization of desire, they almost compulsively reproduce the scene of the
trauma. Today, this is called Post-Traumatic Stress Disorder and it can
be extended to any traumatic experience.

This disconcerting circumstance confirms the primacy in psychic
life of the pleasure principle which until then had never been ques-
tioned, but only controlled by the reality principle. Freud theorized

DOI: 10.4324/9781003474678-2

about it in 1911 in his paper *Formulations on the Two Principles of Mental Functioning*. At the same time, the reality principle is also derived from the pleasure principle, which is forced to postpone, to delay, its realization. Here, however, Freud realizes that we are facing something completely different. On a clinical level, after many years of experience, he notes that many patients oppose healing. They come to therapy ostensibly to recover, whereas in reality they do not want, on an unconscious level, to heal and live in greater well-being. This psychic phenomenon must therefore also refer to something – something internal to the patient of which they are unaware, that does not correspond to or goes *beyond* the pleasure principle. This opposition to healing, which all therapists sooner or later experience, is called "negative therapeutic reaction."

Freud suffers many personal losses in the 1920s. The inter-war influenza epidemic claims the life of his beloved daughter. His friend and benefactor Anton von Freund dies of cancer. In 1919, his pupil the psychoanalyst Victor Tausk commits suicide. However, although some biographers assign importance to these events in the genesis of the conception of the death drive, Freud remains decidedly opposed to this reductive view.[2] Of course, the devastation left by the war dents Freudian confidence in the Enlightenment idea of progress and the domination of reason and, together with the dreams of the traumatized and the phenomena of patient resistance to healing, he is forced to investigate archaic, ancient, anti-vital pulsational motions at work inside humans which do not seem to take into account the pleasure principle.

So why not just theorize an unpleasure principle? The phenomenon, Freud understands, is not that simple. The very title of the essay, always important in Freudian writings, suggests that the theme of pleasure is involved. *Jenseits* (beyond), in fact, is not a negative adverb. It literally means "on the other side," so it is necessary to theorize something that *is not the opposite of pleasure*, but in some way *another* pleasure, a different pleasure completely unconsciously expressed, which Lacan will call *jouissance* or *jouissance mortelle*.[3]

To sum up: the run-up to the 1920s is decisive for Freud in giving theoretical form to certain phenomena that seem inexplicable in light of the normal pleasure principle, as well as the reflections that the devastating Great War brought with it. These phenomena are: the dreams of those who were traumatized by the war; children's play; patient resistance to healing; transference; and repetition. Each of these appears to be mysteriously released from the pleasure principle, which pushes human life forward and guarantees its survival.

It is therefore necessary to put into play the existence of a different principle, hostile to well-being, repetitive. Freud gives this new principle the name "death drive."

The previous path

Although the theorization may be said to have been completed in 1920, as with any Freudian concept, the death drive is the result of a long path of thought that we can see starts from his 1895 book *Project for a Scientific Psychology*.[4] Published posthumously in 1950, this work is considered highly important today with its wealth of intuitions and an object of interest for neuroscience. The essay represents Freud's first attempt to explain psychic phenomena in a neurophysiological way, integrating the physical knowledge of the time with the revolutionary discovery of the unconscious. Freud identifies in the neuronal cell a substantial search for a *lowering of tension*, a push to always return the psychic apparatus to a homeostasis according to the principle of constancy, or inertia (Freud, 1895). The psychic apparatus, incessantly inundated by a continuous drive flow, is constantly engaged in keeping at bay or moderating this tension that would otherwise be overwhelming. I will return to the importance of the *Project for a Scientific Psychology* in Chapter 8, when I will discuss the relationship of the death drive with neuroscience. In this essay, fundamental today in the light of new studies on the death drive, Freud postulates that neurons must handle a certain level of excitement (Q), a *quantity,* and he defines the original tendency of the neuronal system as one of trying to reach a "level=0," the equivalent of a search of a total absence of excitation, or of the fastest possible discharge of the Q quantities to re-establish a level of 0 (Freud, 1895). This is the "first fundamental definition" of *Project for a Scientific Psychology* and it can be considered the basis of all his theoretical construction on the psychic apparatus. Therefore, the seeds of the death drive originate from afar, from the principle of constancy, or inertia[5]: The psychic apparatus cannot withstand excessive disturbances. It seeks to maintain stability. Disturbances are caused by excitement, external and above all internal, and when they are excessive and overwhelm defences, they are called trauma. The psyche must therefore continually try to reduce Q, so as not to be overwhelmed.

Later, in 1911, with his book of papers *Formulations on the Two Principles of Mental Functioning*, the principle of reality's arrival on the scene is a first contribution, necessary for life, to contain the pleasure principle. This is followed in 1915 by *Instincts and Their Vicissitudes* (one of the five *Metapsychology* essays),[6] where we see how one of the destinies of the drive is to convert love into hate. It should be emphasized here that hate is primary and so it appears before love.

In 1915, a decidedly important precursor of the reflections that will appear in *Beyond the Pleasure Principle* is the set of twin essays *Thoughts for Times on War and Death*, where the pessimism emerges about humankind's ability to transform egoistic drives under the influence of Eros, so that we must guard against the illusion of "over-estimating the total susceptibility to culture in comparison with the portion of instinctual life which has remained primitive" (1915, p. 283). Freud takes up these concepts anew in *Civilization and Its Discontents* (1929) and in his correspondence with Einstein in 1932.

Freud mentions "repetition compulsion" for the first time in 1919, just a year before *Beyond the Pleasure Principle*, in *The Uncanny*, an essay of a different nature, as it is dedicated to artistic phenomena. This tendency to repeat plays an important part in the genesis of the uncanny. So, we read in *The Uncanny*:

(...) it is possible to recognize the dominance in the unconscious mind of a '*compulsion to repeat*' proceeding from the instinctual impulses and probably inherent in the very nature of the instincts – a compulsion powerful enough to overrule the pleasure principle, lending to certain aspects of the mind their daemonic character, and still very clearly expressed in the impulses of small children; and compulsion, too, which is responsible for a part of the course taken by the analyses of neurotic patients.

(1919, p. 238)

In this extraordinarily important passage we already find almost all the terms that will form the themes of *Beyond the Pleasure Principle*: The "daemonic" nature of this paradoxical phenomenon called repetition compulsion, its expression in children's play and in the strong resistance we encounter in analysis.

Deconstructing *Beyond the Pleasure Principle* is a worthwhile exercise that yields many fascinating insights.

Beyond the Pleasure Principle: structure of the work

The essay, composed of eight chapters, can be described as dualistic: the first part describes clinical and observational facts:

a   the wooden reel game or, rather, the pleasure of repetition
b   the dreams of those who were traumatized by the Great War
c   repetition compulsion
d   negative therapeutic reaction – the tendency in some patients not to recover or, when they do improve, to regress to a previous stage.

These clinical events lead Freud to conceive of a drive that avoids the pleasure principle, because all these phenomena, present to varying degrees in all of us, manifest themselves via a subjective feeling of sorrow, of pain, and yet they are not removed. To those who accuse this essay of being excessively abstract, I would like to stress that it sprang from the observation of facts that today are easily evident.

The second part, from Chapter 4 onwards, is what Freud called speculative. As we have seen, in complete freedom Freud makes an argumentative leap that is methodologically necessary to explain, in psychoanalytic-biological terms, the mysterious phenomena observed in the first four chapters:

"What follows is speculation, often far-fetched speculation" (1920, p. 606).

This is an utterly paradigmatic leap and it is this leap that makes the essay, which some have called "contradictory," "brilliant" (Deleuze, 1971; Laplanche, 1991), a breakthrough for all psychoanalytic theory, "the real cornerstone of metapsychology" (Couvreur, 1989). Its importance is mainly thanks to its questioning of the fundamental primacy of psychic life, namely the pleasure principle, and the view of psychism as fundamentally dualistic, as it is governed by two antithetical impulses, life and death.

This entails revising his entire drive theory, which in fact Freud ends up designating as the *second theory of impulses*. With so much at stake, Freud, usually a fast writer, takes more than a year to write the text of *Beyond the Pleasure Principle*. He sends it first to the Hungarian psychoanalyst Sándor Ferenczi (1919).[7] The readings of Schopenhauer and Nietzsche were certainly important for Freud, as influences from other authors, although it was not usual for Freud to use philosophers as references. The Nietzschean eternal recurrence theory and its affinity with repetition compulsion[8] is evident; as for Schopenhauer,[9] it is Freud himself who declares that he has arrived at the same outcomes, through other ways, of his philosophy, for whom "death is the 'real result' of life, and therefore in so far its aim" (Freud, 1920, p. 50). The only other text that Freud mentions in a note, but admits he did not understand, is *Destruction as the Cause of Coming into Being* by Sabina Spielrein (1912), one of the first female psychoanalysts, for whom he nevertheless acknowledges gratitude for putting this concept in a nutshell.

In the first chapters Freud describes the seemingly incomprehensible facts that have attracted his attention. Let us look at them.

Clinical observations

The first fact is new and fundamental, "traumatic neurosis," which can be widely observed in war veterans; their dreams, which continually repeat the traumatic event, do not respond to the theory of desire in the dream, for there is no desire or pleasure to be found in returning to the trauma. One would expect they would dream of the time before the trauma, but these former soldiers masochistically dream of the very event that made them suffer. This was a time of great interest in war neuroses, so much so that a conference was held just before the end of the Great War, where not only psychoanalysts but also military psychiatrists addressed the subject. What kind of trauma is it? While it is certainly not a sexual trauma, Freud is led to believe that even the external event, if excessive for the psyche, can be treated as an internal event where "the mechanical force of the trauma would set free the quota of sexual excitement which, in consequence of the lacking preparation by apprehension, has a traumatic effect" (1920, p. 33). Psychologically, trauma is akin to breaking and entering, a violent breach of the protective barrier, whether it is internal or external. More generally, it is something that overcomes the containing capabilities of the psychic apparatus. These days we could view the repetition of traumatic dreams also as an attempt to process trauma, to represent it in order to cope with it, although that is not always the case. In David's case, which I will describe later, we have a patient stuck in a traumatic dream that doesn't seem to lend itself to psychic processing.

The second point concerns children's play. It is derived from Freud's famous observation of his grandson Ernst. In the absence of his mother, the child invents a game, which will be called the reel game, in which he throws a cotton reel repeatedly back and forth, alternating disappearance with reappearance. Two observations are fundamental in this game: the first is to note "the great achievement of civilization achieved by the child, and that is the drive renunciation" (ibid., p. 201), through which the child dominates and manages his mother's absence, thus transforming an unpleasant and passive event into something active that he now dominates. We observe this reversal on numerous occasions in life and in our clinical work, where the patient often tends to escape the relative passivity that analytical care entails, trying to be the one who holds the strings.

Freud's other ingenious intuition is to observe repetition. He understands that it is not so much the object of repetition that brings pleasure to the child but the very act of repetition. Contrary to what one would expect, namely that pleasure is given by novelty, seemingly useless repetition itself gives the pleasure of dominating the trauma (maternal absence), of binding[10] on a metapsychological level, free energy that would otherwise be destructive, excessive, and thus the child acquires a kind of pleasure *(jenseits,* another pleasure). We read in Freud,

> In the case of children's play (…) Novelty is always the condition of enjoyment. But children will never tire of asking an adult to repeat a game that he has shown them or played with them (…) None of this contradicts the pleasure principle; *repetition, the re-experiencing of something identical, it is clearly in itself a source of pleasure.* In the case of a person in analysis, on the contrary, the compulsion to repeat the events of his childhood in the transference evidently disregards the pleasure principle in every way. The patient behaves in a purely infantile fashion and thus shows us that the repressed memory-traces of his more primaeval experiences are not present in him in a bound state.
>
> (ibid., 1920, pp. 611–612, my italics)

We therefore see the two sides of repetition compulsion: on the one hand, as in children's play, the pleasure principle can serve; on the other hand, as in the case of transference, and especially in negative transference, it does cause displeasure. Yet the person does not free himself of it. The next theoretical step is this:

> But how is the predicate of being 'instinctual' – Freud asks – related to the compulsion to repeat? At this point we cannot escape

a suspicion that we may have come upon the track of a universal attribute of instincts, and perhaps of organic life in general (...) *an instinct is an urge inherent in the organic life to restore an earlier state of things* which the living entity has been obliged to abandon under the pressure of external disturbing forces.

(ibid., 1920, p. 612)

The drive movement tends to return, to repeat what has been lived. Freud has already theorized the conservative nature of the drives in his essay *On Narcissism* (1914), six years before *Beyond the Pleasure Principle*, distinguishing between life or libidinal drives and self-preservation drives, but these will then merge into the death drive. This first and important stage of *On Narcissism* shows how Freud has always had in mind the conservative nature of the drives, so much so that, he will say in his book *Moses and Monotheism* many years later, "What has once come to life clings tenaciously to its existence. One feels inclined to doubt sometimes whether the dragons of primaeval days are really extinct" (1939, p. 229).

We can admire just how well artists know how to grasp the profound nature of the human psyche with Milan Kundera (who opens *The Unbearable Lightness of Being* with the theory of eternal return):

"Human time does not turn in a circle; it runs ahead in a straight line. That is why man cannot be happy: *happiness is the longing for repetition*" (1984, p. 298, my italics).

Even in clinical experience, we constantly observe how, not only in transference, the patient is induced to repeat a coaction which, Freud says, probably could not express itself prior to therapeutic work loosening the removal. But repetition compulsion – this unconscious internal push that leads us to return to the scene of the crime, repeating exactly what it made us suffer – extends far beyond the therapeutic relationship: it affects and sometimes ruins our whole lives. Some people who seem to be haunted by fate, they always run into the same trouble, as if caught up in something "daemonic" (Freud, 1920, p. 612), in an eternal return of the same; these are the so-called fate neuroses, familiar to us all. It follows that the only conclusion is that "there really does exist in the mind a compulsion to repeat which overrides the pleasure principle" (ibid., p. 605). Freud ends the third chapter by writing that this compulsion "seems more primitive, more elementary, more instinctual than the pleasure principle which it over-rides" (ibid., p. 605).

Analytical treatment also tries to bind the drive, for example in transference; especially at the beginning, during the honeymoon phase when the patient often improves (and then often worsens again) due mainly to the investment made in the therapist, an emotional investment that, on a metapsychological level, binds energy. The phenomenon of positive transference as a vehicle for improvement and healing also occurs in medicine, where it is said that "the doctor is the best medicine."

Chapter 4 and onward: speculation

Starting from Chapter 4, the so-called speculative part begins:

> What follows – he writes – is speculation, often far-fetched speculation, which the reader will consider or dismiss according to his individual predilection. It is further an attempt to follow out an idea consistently, out of curiosity to see where it will lead.
>
> (1920, p. 606)

Thus, entrusting the reader with the curiosity or otherwise to follow him in this exploration, Freud hypothesizes that the living substance was born at some point through a sort of tension or imbalance, thus creating a trauma and rendering the living substance dominated by the tendency to cancel that imbalance in order to return to the primitive state of quiet. He more fully explores the considerations previously seen in *Project for a Scientific Psychology*, including the fundamental Constancy Principle.[11] To this state, one can also give the suggestive name of Nirvana (or the Nirvana principle), which literally means to exhale a breath or to extinguish, a term taken from Eastern religions which represents the highest state of peace.[12] Living is therefore an anxiety brought about by sexual or life drives, which sometimes, if perceived as excessive or disturbing, must be silenced. The second type of impulses are called the death drives (*Todestrieb*) to distinguish them from the life or libido drives. The impulses of life are erotic, they push to live, to create bonds and connections; while the impulses of death tend to untie, disconnect, cancel. It is as if life always tended to return to its beginning, to a before, which we can only imagine, but which is the reason for this push, present in human beings through these phenomena listed by Freud, towards self-destruction. If, for the death drives, Freud invokes the Nirvana principle, of total quiet, for the life drives he refers to Plato, who in the Symposium imagines that at the beginning of mankind Zeus cut the human being in two, and since then each half has been seeking its lost other half: this is the nature of Eros.

It is certainly a shocking text, because it assumes within human nature an innate ability to destroy itself, as if "the organism wishes to die only in its own fashion" (ibid., p. 614).

This property of the drive is universal and, by Freud's own admission, makes the very definition of "drive" difficult because until now it has identified as a drive something that drives us forward, "whereas we are now asked to recognize in them the precise contrary – an expression of the conservative nature of living substance (…) the elementary living entity would from its very beginning have had no wish to change" (ibid., pp. 612–613).

Does it follow that progress is an illusion? That everything returns to the past? That we are victims of ineffable, ontological nostalgia?

The French psychoanalyst Jacques Lacan (1959–1960), who, as we will see, will fully accept the notion of a death drive, and indeed make it the only drive, says that no text, such as *Beyond the Pleasure Principle*, would so thoroughly challenge the very idea of progress. What is even more scandalous is that all of this, as the title says, does not happen without a quota, naturally unconscious, of pleasure.

In his acclaimed biography of Freud, Peter Gay points out four reasons why this essay is difficult to read: a prose that does not show Freud's usual lucidity and requires the understanding of new ideas in extremely condensed passages; Freud's launching so freely into flights of fantasy; the loss of the reassuring familiarity with the clinical experience which characterizes Freudian texts; and, finally, the fact that Freud here would push his usual protest of uncertainty to an unprecedented extent (Gay, 1988). These are the very same elements which for others, myself included, are instead elements of merit!

It is important to point out that, in the spirit of a true researcher, Freud may always potentially challenge all his own speculations; this also applies to the death drive, of which he will write to his friend and colleague Ernest Jones, "naturally, all this is groping speculation, until one has something better" (1935).[13]

Repetition compulsion: Mrs G.
and the assembly line

Mrs. G. is 62 years old. She is a sensitive and intelligent woman, who asks for a fourth analysis because she is very unhappy, in despair over her tormented love life. The three previous analyses did not last more than two years because Mrs. G. was always disappointed. The first analyst was "too rigid" for her. In the second case a psychologist gave her advice that, in her opinion, proved not to be appropriate. With the third analyst, shortly before she consulted me, she developed a strong erotic transference which obviously caused the interruption of the analysis.

Mrs. G. has been married twice. Although she has a degree in psychology she works as a teacher. Especially in recent years, she is scared by the passage of time. She engages in numerous sexual relationships to a promiscuous degree, usually with men she meets on the Internet. She asks for my help precisely because with the most recent of these, M., she has plunged again into the depression that has haunted her since adolescence. It emerges, already during our initial conversations, that her mother was severely depressed and her father was often absent because he worked on ships. G., an only daughter, spent long periods with her depressed mother, waiting with joy for her father's arrival, who brought some relief, with his gifts and new stories to tell. During these exchanges it becomes clear that Mrs. G., increasingly over time, seeks a balm in her love affairs, as I tell her. She uses sex to relieve her depression, repeating, in an increasingly desperate way, her childhood pattern. She is a prisoner of repetition compulsion.

Her last lover, M., neglects her, does not call her, callously makes her wait for him only to then disappear. "But when he comes back," says the patient, "I feel reborn, I come back to life, even if I know it is an illusion, that then the cycle will repeat itself." She understands that even with her most recent analyst the cycle had repeated itself: it had made her "fall in love" and feel excited to avoid dealing with her underlying depression. We know that erotized transfer constitutes a strong resistance.[14]

As often happens in these cases, when she meets a man who loves her in a tranquil relationship devoid of exciting shocks, Mrs. G. soon gets fed up. Because of the compulsion to repeat, this woman, while capable of insight, repeats the trauma: to escape from depression, probably caused by infantile identification with the depressed mother, she seeks the pleasure of the father's return, transformed today into the intoxication of sexual encounters. I will not go into the merits of the case, which I mention here only for the part that interests us, namely the repetition, but it is clear that not only was G. not considered by a depressed mother, but she also had to take care of her too; the father, on the other hand, seemed to be coming back "just for her." At the same time, Mrs. G. understands that this is leading her to self-destruction.

She tells me that in a dream she meets a man, "I don't know who, one of those I meet on Tinder. We make love, I'm on top of him, and then there's a bad scene… it seems like he's pulling my leg off."

She associates that the man could be the last one she met on one of these dates and she had not liked him at all, she just wanted "not to think," and she doesn't understand why her body comes disassembled, as if on an "assembly line." We understand together how this mechanical sexuality, made up of pieces, partial objects, where she is not considered nor regards the other as a person, makes it anonymous as on an assembly line, and exposes her to continuous repetition.

The dream allows her to better understand how she feels trapped, alienated by the infinite series of assembly line repetition, in this case mechanical and anonymizing, just the opposite of what she is trying to achieve from these encounters. It is not a traumatic dream in the sense described in *Beyond the Pleasure Principle* such as those of war veterans, or as we will see with David, but a dream offered for elaboration, which repeats in the hope that analytical listening will collect and process it.

Notes

1 It is important to note the German title of the work, *Jenseits des Lustprinzips.*

2 In particular, Freud's first biographer, Fritz Wittels, in 1924 gave importance to these losses, which actually took place before 1920.

3 Lacan J. (1959–1960): *The Seminar of Jacques Lacan, Book VII, The Ethics of Psychoanalysis.* Turin, Einaudi, 1994.

4 The "Project for a Scientific Psychology" – a title provided by the editors upon the manuscript's first publication in 1950 – is part of Freud's correspondence with Wilhelm Fliess. His two aims in this piece were to arrive at "a sort of economics of nerve forces" and "to peel off from psychopathology a gain for normal psychology" (Freud to Fliess, May 25, 1895, p. 129). Freud's "Project" was first conceived in late March, 1895 and, in September, returning from a visit to Fliess in Berlin, where the two discussed it, he begins the writing. On October 8, he sends Fliess two notebooks, holding back a third dealing with repression. Even at this time

Freud oscillates between feeling that the work we know as the "Project" was "delusional" and feeling that it was an excellent start on "the elucidation of the neuroses;" and if the "quantitative conception" would in fact never disappear from his work, it would always remain in the background.

5 The two terms are often used interchangeably, as Freud argues that the principle of inertia aims to discharge tension and restore the minimum energy condition, suggesting that within the physiological functioning there are circuits whose function is to maintain homeostasis. However, there are some who tend to separate them (Than The et al., 2020), but I do not think this distinction is necessary. I will therefore refer to the principle of constancy or inertia.

6 *Metapsychology* is a group of essays which Freud wrote in a specific creative impetus in 1915. They were initially supposed to be 12 but, for reasons unknown, he retained only five: *Repression, Mourning and Melancholia, Instincts and Their Vicissitudes, The Unconscious, A Metapsychological Supplement to the Theory of Dreams*.

7 Freud to Ferenczi, March 28 and 31, 1919.

8 Nietzsche first considers eternal recurrence in *The Gay Science* in 1882.

9 In *The World as Will and Representation* in 1818. Freud always acknowledges psychoanalysis' debt to Schopenhauer, the first philosopher to conceive the concepts of the unconscious, of the conflicting nature of humankind, of unhappiness as an inevitable human destiny, and of the need to renounce, in other words, for sublimation.

10 The notion of free or bound energy comes from Freud's early studies with Josef Breuer (1895) and Freud never abandoned it. It means that the libidinal energy crosses these two states, and that in repetition compulsion (being bound) displeasure is managed. Free energy corresponds to the primary process (a dream, for example) and is bound to the secondary process (a thought, for example).

11 The Constancy Principle, or principle of constancy, is also called the principle of inertia.

12 Barbara Low, one of the first British psychoanalysts, introduces the term Nirvana in 1920. That same year, Freud writes about it in *Beyond the Pleasure Principle*. In Japanese literature, including contemporary, it is found as a name that ancient Japanese monks gave to a temple in which they were buried alive in the placid expectation of death. This live immurement represents the Freudian death drive well.

13 Freud to Jones, March 3, 1935.

14 On the subject there is extensive literature starting with Freud, 1914 (*Observations on Transference-Love*). I recommend: Bolognini S. (1994); Blum H.P. (1973); Wallerstein R.S. (1993); and Isolan L.R. (2005).

Chapter 2

Death wish or death of desire?

Open questions

The Freudian death drive raises several questions on the theoretical level. French authors are in the main responsible for deepening Freud's thinking. Through them, the death drive finds definitions such as the "denied desire" (Julia Kristeva, 2005). Here, even more intriguing questions and aporias emerge: if, strictly speaking, the death drive does not correspond to the desire to die, then what desire is it? What drive is it? And, more to the point, can we still talk about drive?

One could summarize the questions raised by the death drive as follows: (a) was it really a necessary concept? (b) how can the leap from biological to metapsychology be explained? (c) why label such a tendency with the word death if it is also necessary for psychic life? (Penot, 2006).

These are not questions which require a straightforward concrete answer but, in my opinion, they do open up interesting scenarios. To speak of a desire for death, in the Freudian understanding, would, however, be rather inaccurate: Freud has always argued that there can be a death *"anguish"* in a person (Freud, 1926), but not a desire in the strict sense, because death is unrepresentable for the unconscious; death, that is, does not exist for the unconscious, only its anguish can exist (Freud, 1926). With regard to suicide, the death one can procure for oneself, as described in the admirable essay *Mourning and Melancholia* (1915), can exist only – and this is above all the case of the melancholic – when the Ego treats itself as an object, so that suicide would ultimately be murder: in order to eliminate the bad object I have introjected, I must kill myself, too. The death drive we are dealing with here has nothing to do with either death anguish or suicide in the strict

DOI: 10.4324/9781003474678-3

sense, even if on a clinical level it can then express itself as death of the individual as well, who in the end has exhausted all his desire, his vital charge. In my opinion, it is something that we observe very clearly in all kinds of addiction or substance abuse. Addicts can activate death, as sometimes happens, but their first desire is to "stop thinking," to forget: "*I want to switch my brain off,*" a substance-addicted patient of mine used to say. Their foremost desire is pleasure or, rather, to avoid unpleasure. We will return to addictions later.[1]

So what does death of desire mean? *Beyond the Pleasure Principle*, which as we have seen, is rich in genius and contradictions, which does not conclude and "which never abdicates" (Lacan, 1954), already in its title calls into question the relationships between pleasure and something that overcomes it. The death of desire seems to correspond to the ultimate goal of the drive which, after it runs its course, tends to the extinction of desire. It is worth recalling briefly that the drive, the boundary concept between psychic and somatic as Freud has always defined it, recognizes a *source*, an *aim* and an *object* (Freud, 1915b).

But what are the source, aim and object of the death drive? We can recognize the aim and object in the death of desire, in Nirvana, in the shutdown of all the excitement and disturbance they cause (principle of constancy or inertia). These same excitations, coming from within the organism as from the outside, can generically be the source. Therefore, I hypothesize that Freud did worry about finding another name for the death drive as it makes a counterbalance to the life drive and because it responds to the drive criteria in general: it consists of a source, an aim and an object. If death is its end, understood as the death of desire, then it can be said that all drives tend to this, that *every drive is, in the end, the death drive*. This is the thesis that Lacan later argues – that there is only one drive and it is the death drive. Personally, I prefer to remain in the Freudian vein which instead provides for pulsional dualism, death and life, and their continuous mixing (which Freud calls *fusion* and *defusion*), although I recognize the validity of the Lacanian venture: if we are to die, all of the drive in the end can be interpreted as death's.

Linguistic note

It is important to insert a footnote on language. In order to understand not only the death drive, but the concept of the drive in general, we must be careful with the translations that, at times, have caused a lot of confusion. Death drive is the German translation of *Todertrieb*. Freud uses the German term *Trieb*, from the verb *trieben* (to push), precisely to indicate the pulsional flow's character of *push, of urgency* that constantly inhabits us (in French *pulsion*, in Italian *pulsione,* in Spanish *pulsion*). This should not be confused with *instinct*, which has sometimes been used or translated, for example in Kleinian writing. Drive and instinct have nothing in common. Instinct, typical of the animal, involves predetermined and ethologically defined behaviours, while the drive is unpredictable, bizarre, always excessive and exclusively human. In the most recent English translations, *drive* has finally been chosen to indicate the *push* that characterizes the drive, an element which is completely lacking in instinct.

Even more complex is the translation of *pleasure.* The German title, *Jenseits des Lustprinzips,* uses the ambiguous term *Lust,* meaning both "pleasure" and what some call "desire," or *libido,* but what for Freud is always tension, unpleasure. In German, *Lust* has an erotic implication that is not found in the English *pleasure.* In a polysemantic way it means desire and pleasure, concupiscence and enjoyment. *Lust* is not only pleasure, but it incites one towards pleasure and would therefore imply pleasure-unpleasure *("Unlust"),* because after 1920, from a psychoanalytic point of view, it is no longer possible to consider pleasure only as the classic pleasure tied to discharge, as understood in Project for a Scientific Psychology (1895). Due to the term's ambiguity, Freud is initially reluctant to use it. After proposing the term libido in *Three Essays on the Theory of Sexuality* (1905), he adds in a 1910 note that "the only appropriate word in the German language, Lust, is unfortunately ambiguous, and used to denote the experience both of a need (*Bedurfnis*) and of a gratification (*Befriedigung*)." Yet everything led us to believe that Freud later adopted the term not despite its ambiguity, but actually because of it.

For Freud pleasure is equal to a reduction or annulment of unpleasure (also known as displeasure), and unpleasure is thus unfulfilled desire (*Trieb*, drive, libido). However, in his idea of things, pleasure and unpleasure are effects of *Lust because it is an essential cause of psychic life:* unpleasure corresponds to an increase and pleasure to a decrease in the amount of free energy. When satisfaction is selfish, it is perceived by the Ego as *Unlust;* for example, neurotic symptoms, persecutory thoughts, or anxiety dreams produce *Unlust* in the Ego. *Lust* manifests itself in the Ego with its double face, not just one as *Lust but also as Unlust.*

In short, the pleasure principle leads to feelings that are both pleasant and unpleasant for the Ego. If we used Aristotelian terminology, we could say that pleasure is the ultimate cause of any psychic process and unpleasure is not. For Freud, pleasure can be equated to the reduction or annulment of unpleasure, and unpleasure is thus unsatisfied desire. This also means that unpleasure for the Ego – the effect of the conflict between instincts and even *Unlust* – can become an end in itself. This becomes of vital importance in masochism, as we will see.

The concept of pleasure in human beings is thus much more complex and related to sorrow, that is, to death.

A thousand faces of Thanatos: what is pleasure?

> The pleasure principle, though it may rule over all, does not have the final or highest authority over all. There are no exceptions to the principle, but there is a residue that is irreducible to it; nothing contradicts the principle, but there remains something external which falls outside it and is not homogeneous with it.
>
> (Deleuze, 1971, p. 98)

Although the concept of the death of desire may seem abstract and elusive, there are many expressions of it, not only in the clinic but in life in general. André Green writes, "What does the Ego want? That you leave it in peace" (1990).

Think of the hikikomori that has spread from Japan to other continents since the 1980s. The term means "to stand aside" and it describes the young people, mostly teenagers, who do not actively commit suicide (which would be a desire for death), but who withdraw completely from the world and social life, staying in their rooms, sometimes for years, connected to their PlayStations or computers, thus achieving a total suspension of desire, a zeroing of the urge or thrust to act and to desire.[2] These young recluses clearly achieve the Nirvana of Japanese monks, *they are walled up alive* to avoid the suffering and turbulence that desire causes and the fatigue of development. Paradoxically, the act of suicide would have involved a desire, a quota of Eros necessary to self-destruct.

The same Nirvanic state exists in addiction, which perhaps represent the paradigm of the contemporary clinic. Even in the throes of addiction the individual does not generally actively procure death but through the object of his dependency reaches a state of imperturbability, extinguishing all internal tensions, not just the unpleasant but also the pleasant. All of us, to varying degrees throughout our lives, go through stages in which we seek peace, in which our Ego, as Green says, would only like to "be left alone." But generally this blends in with the permanence of some push of desire. The death drive, therefore, does not necessarily aim to annul life, but the internal tensions, the excitement, that *desire*, as Kristeva (2005) writes, which conceivably did not exist before the birth of life and belongs to a mythical "before life."

Here we are resolutely at the very edge of psychoanalysis, as well as face to face with considerations on human nature. No text like this has gone so far in trying to understand, between the psychic and the biological, the mystery of human pleasure, which always involves a quota of unpleasure. Some suggest, in fact, that the title could have been "pleasure-unpleasure principle" ("Lust-Unlust"), in that pleasure is always other than self (Benvenuto, 2003). The pleasure of repetition is not the same pleasure as that produced by the discharge of sexual tension, for example, nor is masochistic pleasure which, as we will see, is steeped in pain. This facet of pleasure in humankind makes us understand how difficult it is for the clinician to recognize the 1,000 faces of Thanatos; faces that, moreover, act in silence:

"(...) we are driven to conclude that the death instincts are by their nature mute, and that the clamour of life proceeds for the most part from Eros" (Freud, 1923, p. 46).

A clinical case: David and his retreat

I meet David when he's 18 and supposed to be in his final year of high school. His parents consult me because they are very concerned about him. At the beginning of the school year, David barricaded himself inside his room and won't let anyone in. He has gone so far as to seal the door with towels. However, he agrees to talk to me. Given that he refuses to leave the house, I suggest we start by using Skype. So begins a therapy that is now in its third year of two sessions a week. After the first year, David manages to come to the sessions in person, face to face, because I think he needs the sensory attachment of the therapist's vision and on the couch he would be too distressed and, in any case, given the extreme poverty of his capacity for representation, unable to produce free association.

To all appearances a handsome, sporty and intelligent boy, David is on the edge of the hikikomori. His existence takes place in social retreat. He tells of a life marked by trauma, particularly in school. He was bullied in primary school, was perpetually isolated and always felt different from the others until high school, a time he refuses to remember so intense is his terror, where he was targeted by a teacher, not supported by anyone and not understood by parents who, according to him, underestimated the problem. Alongside frequent hypochondriac symptoms that allowed him to stay home from school, while sometimes fantasizing about committing suicide by jumping out of a window at school, David chose to *stop wanting and desiring*: His life has become increasingly poorer, both in terms of acquaintances and activities, but above all within his mind. There are no dreams, except for a tiny handful of traumatic dreams such as those Freud describes in *Beyond the Pleasure Principle*: he is inside the classroom and hears his classmates talking behind his back, or he is in the classroom in total darkness, distressed and lost.

Like the First World War veterans in Freud's writings, David relives the trauma scenes. It seems he doesn't know how to, nor does he want to, detach himself from them. His classmates' bullying, to which his shyness was unable to react, has caused an irreparable narcissistic wound so that today David defends himself with retreat and an almost paranoid mistrust, accepting contact only with his family members, the few people he trusts and with me.

In some sessions he acknowledges that he wants to keep his mind "off." In the early days, he used to say: "*I don't want to think, don't make me think, I just want to forget.*" I suppose the patient has structured a psychopathology of the kind that Green calls "état limite," to be placed within a "clinic of the negative," which we frequently come across nowadays (Green, 1993). As the term says, these are states at the limit of thinkability and also at the limit of indications for psychoanalysis. They should not be confused with borderline states, where, on the contrary, patients frequently experience anger and other very intense feelings. David, on the other hand, not feeling equipped to face the complexity of life, to wit desire, has zeroed it. But the fact that he comes to the sessions and maintains a relationship with me is an indication that this "attack on linking" (Bion, 1959), this tendency to the death of desire, is not total. From another point of view, David is one of those patients Steiner (1993) describes as having built "psychic retreats," inner fortresses where they are sheltered from persecutory and depressive anxieties, but everything always happens with substantial suffering.

I believe the analyst's task here is to free the patient, slowly due to the marked narcissistic fragility, from the tendency to slip into a framework of pure unpleasure. I try to help David regain confidence in the *word* as a metaphorical means by which to describe his internal state and to structure a more solid personality. At present, David has not returned to his studies, which still terrify him, but he has taken up the sport he is very good at again, he can train by himself, he derives an important narcissistic return from it and no one humiliates him. Albeit limited to this area, which he feels is under his control, he does seem to have mobilized some desire, some Eros.

Although David's traumatic dreams don't lend themselves to real interpretations, I still tried to use them as the only unconscious material that he has provided, showing him how, by constantly repeating the traumatic scene within himself, he is also unconsciously trying to relive it not just to suffer but also to try to prevail over it. In conclusion, as I see things, I am inclined to consider David's state as a "death narcissism" (Green, 1983), in an *état limite* personality, where the patient defends himself from the psychic suffering he found unbearable, cancelling any libidinal investment, be it in himself (with the consequence of always feeling empty) or in the outside world. This is the clinic of *disinvestment* (Valdrè, 2019), which we can read as an expression of the death drive. There are states that can be confused with depressive states. In fact, before David consults me, he is prescribed antidepressants, without success. Depression's classic themes of guilt and unworthiness are not to be found if a depressive experience exists, as is the case with David. His depression is connected and secondary to the vacuum both inside and outside of himself, the result of desertification by disinvestment. In addition, great narcissistic fragility is often unconsciously compensated for by grandiose ideas, in David's case with the idea of becoming a great champion in his beloved sport.[3]

Notes

1 See Loose R. (2005) for a review of the problem of drug addiction: *The Addicted Subject caught between the Ego and the Drive: The post-Freudian Reduction and Simplification of a Complex Clinical Problem.* Psychoanalytische Perspectieven No. 41/42.

2 The documentary *Web Junkie* (by Hilla Medalia and Shosh Shlam, 2013), describes the first Chinese hospital for the treatment of internet addiction, for adolescents suffering from this type of severe retreat.

3 These narcissistic states can also partially fit Kohut's description of the grandiose Self (Kohut, 1971, 1977).

Chapter 3

A controversial concept

The death drive in the post-Freud era

When a concept appears so divisive in psychoanalysis, in my opinion, it is not merely due to theoretical or technical reasons, it must obviously touch on something disturbing: there is a *scandal* in the death drive, the idea that life does not tend to the Good. Moreover, for the first time in psychoanalysis, death not only loses that aura of abstraction with which philosophy has always imbued it, but *it is placed in the body*, within us, like pulsional baggage we carry inside us.

It is understandable that an idea of this kind may be enthusiastically welcomed as a brilliant intuition, or with distrust, or with disquiet. Having said that, the post-Freudian panorama can be divided into three groupings: those who, following in Freud's footsteps, accept the concept and deepen it; those who partially accept it primarily on a clinical level; and those who do not show interest and keep away from it. Psychoanalysts who consider themselves Freudian believe that the death drive is a relevant idea; the French, the Lacanian and some post-Kleinian thinkers such as Otto Kernberg belong to this group. However, for them (the Kleinians in particular) the death drive has become a clinical fact that influences the way of working in the clinic.

French psychoanalysis

In the first group are some of Freud's earliest contemporaries, especially the group closest to him (Fenichel, 1945; Deutsch, 1965),[1] but most notably the vast group of French psychoanalysts or those within the Francophone influence (which includes not only France, but part of Italy, Canada and Latin America). There are small differences even among these.

DOI: 10.4324/9781003474678-4

One of the most significant authors, and one who has been most concerned with the subject, Jean Laplanche, recognizes the existence of a death drive, but still makes it derive from Eros. For him, there is *only one* sexual drive, from which everything originates, which later is distinguished in the sexual drive of life and sexual drive of death (Laplanche, 1970). Only the sexual death drive corresponds to the "un-linked" aspect and is therefore dangerous in relation to life, that is, it is a deadly current that, even if it emanates from the sexual (*sexuale*, as he defines it),[2] can be detached from it. Laplanche does not see the existence of an autonomous death drive but recognizes it as a devia-tion from sexuality. The death of the Ego can occur in two ways, either through the invasion of an unbound sexual drive or through the avoid-ance of all tensions by the narcissistic or Nirvanic Ego (this second point is very similar to Andrè Green's "death narcissism"). I do not find this differentiation particularly significant, while Green's differen-tiation between *life narcissism and death narcissism* is more useful and important, especially on a clinical level (1983).

Green's distinction, in my opinion, is to have synthesized the long-standing question between drive and object (already present in Freud) because in death narcissism, quite frequently seen in the clinic as in David's case, sexuality disconnects from the object and becomes what Green calls *de-objectivising*, as opposed to drives that instead maintain their relationship with the object, and are described as *objectivising*.

Therefore, for Green, the death drive is articulated with narcissism: we have "life" narcissism when the link with objects is maintained and "death" narcissism when this link is destroyed. This theoretical differen-tiation becomes very important in the clinic, where Green identifies pa-thologies called "état limite." These are part of the interesting concept of *negative* and *white psychosis* (1990, 1993). In these psychopathological frameworks, we are faced neither with neurotic conflict nor with tradi-tional psychosis, such as schizophrenia, nor with depressive frameworks. In fact, when depressive feelings arise, which generally scare the patient, it means that the therapeutic work is chipping away at the death narcis-sism. These are very delicate clinical moments because they can prompt an interruption or a regression. We are faced with an increasingly wide array of patients (such as David) who experience feelings of emptiness, of non-existence, of a lack of sense. As mentioned before, the best term I would use to describe these mental states is *disinvestment* (Valdrè, 2019). These are patients who cannot invest libidinally in themselves – hence the profound feeling of emptiness – nor in the outside world, therapist

included. This destructive narcissism is, in fact, the basis of many negative therapeutic reactions and finds its theoretical foundation precisely
in the existence of the death drive. Green's originality primarily lies in
his having been able to make the death drive a living concept that acts
in the clinic and in life, where objectivising and de-objectivising drives
alternate, depending on whether the link with the objects is maintained.

Perhaps this is a less pessimistic view than the Freudian one,
because analytical work and transfer can shift erotic libido to other
objects, and in his opinion not all analytical failures are related to the
death drive. Ultimately, to save life, object love remains the fundamental goal, but he agrees with Freud that it is narcissism, or "life
narcissism" – good narcissism, which is commonly identified with
good self-esteem and self-love – that safeguards the Ego's strength.

Roussillon (2000), one of the most significant of the contemporary
authors, speaks of non-differentiation as a function of the death drive.
There is death where the undifferentiated prevails, where differences,
discards are annulled, and then there remains only room for the repetition of the identical. Death, for him, is intrinsic to the drive, and it
is not necessary to have drive dualism: "(…) when the drive tends to
reproduce the identical, whether it is libido or destructiveness, it is
the death drive" (in Doninotti, 2011, p. 85, translated for this edition).

Widlöcher, in 1984, was responsible for the synthesis at the 1986
European Psychoanalytical Federation Congress. Elements of conver-
gence between the various speakers are a certain departure from the biological model and the importance of the *binding* and *unbinding* terms
(which Freud called *fusion and defusion*) to indicate respectively the
maintenance of the bond not only between drives but between drives
and objects, or their breakup leading to their drift towards the death
drive. Among the differences lies the vision of primary narcissism,
which the French maintain in the Freudian sense, while for Segal it is
an expression of the death drive.

Other significant contemporary thinkers, such as Pontalis, Le Guen,
Ribas, Penot, Kristeva and others, have substantially deepened the
Freudian death drive but without making any significant changes.

The shift: the school of object relations

Others among Freud's early collaborators, such as Abraham and
Ferenczi, find the death drive perplexing. In his final papers, Ferenczi
tries to re-introduce the significance of trauma, which he views as

connected to death not as a source but as an outcome: "trauma is a process of dissolution that moves towards total dissolution, that is to say, to death" (Ferenczi, 1995, p. 130). Later, even in unpublished writings (Ferenczi, 1929), he considers the death drive as too pessimistic. Ferenczi's ideas are later rediscovered and reassessed as important regarding trauma theory.

With Melanie Klein and her followers begins a departure from the interest in metapsychology and, consequently, from the death drive. The psychoanalytic orientation that begins with her, which is called the school of object relations, as the term puts it, shifts the emphasis more towards the vicissitudes of the relationship with the object, rather than the internal drive movement.

Outside the Freudian metapsychological framework, that is, the drive theory, it is difficult to place the death drive, so it will be understood as something clinically similar but substantially different. It must be said that, initially at least, Klein and her school accept the concept of the death drive. Indeed it is made a strong point of clinical action, but with her it becomes an eminently clinical concept and one that overlaps with *primary envy* (1957). So here we are talking about a *shift*. There has been an outright shift that no longer retains the Freudian spirit. From a clinical point of view, however, the Kleinian school is credited with trying to use the death drive to bring it to the heart of the clinic. Klein and her followers generally speak of *instinct*, which, as we have seen, does not correspond at all to the concept of drive. For her, the death instinct serves to explain the precocity and severity of the archaic super-ego (a hypothesis that counters both Freud and his daughter Anna) and the envious attack on the maternal breast and all that is good in it represents the maximum expression of destructiveness.

In the same position are the main authors of the Kleinian school, such as Hanna Segal (1993), who points out that she disagrees with the translation of *Trieb* into *instinct* and uses the word *drive*. It is my view that there is an unmistakeable closeness and resonance with the Freudian death drive in the patients that she describes as close to "near death" in an important article of hers, *Addiction to near death* in 1982.

Even Rosenfeld (1975), although starting from Freud, focuses in particular on the clinic, where he finds that not only in personality can there exist an internal force aimed at destruction, but *an organization*, a real *band*, can attack the good parts of the Ego. Here, too, the concept of the death drive is inherent between the lines, but it is mainly evident clinically.

Since the 1980s, the resumption of interest in the death drive, on the part of not only the French, is testified by the First Congress of the European Psychoanalytical Federation in 1984, as previously mentioned, which had as its theme *"The death drive today: a necessary metapsychological concept?"* and where Laplanche, Green, Segal and Widlöcher, in particular, put forward[3] their contrasting views.

David Bell (2015) reports a revival of interest in contemporary post-Kleinians. He recognizes in them three substantial positions: one traditionally related to primary envy; one relatively indifferent; and one, which instead approaches Freudian thought, which speaks of "Nirvana-like" states.

Even Feldman, while retaining the term *instinct*, hypothesizes the existence of an instinctive force towards death, intensely destructive, palpably present in many of our patients, which he calls "forever dying." He discusses the clinical aspects of this force which leads to the patient's unconscious gratification, and therefore is difficult to eliminate. What is "deadly" is the specificity of the attack on mental differences and processes, capable of destroying the patient's vitality as well as their objects. The importance of these "anti-life" impulses is not to kill literally, but "the patient feels impelled to maintain a link with the object that often has an evidently tormenting quality (...) the objects are not dead, but poisoned, weakened, immobilized and, one suspects, forever dying" (2000, pp. 53–56).

In my opinion, these contemporary post-Kleinian authors may change the terms, but the substance is very similar to the Freudian death drive, or Green's "death narcissism."

With Winnicott, the role of the environment and its deficits becomes primary compared to internal drives. Winnicott, Meltzer and Bion, among others, while placing great emphasis on the destructive components of personality in their theories, do not feel the need to make it a specific metapsychological concept, and tend to abandon the Kleinian accent and its innatism as well. The environment, in short, the mother's primary care, her ability to be "good enough," capable of "holding and handling" or, in Bion's terms, her capacity for "reverie" with the child, take on an absolutely prevalent aspect, and it is evident that all this overshadows the existence of a death drive within the individual (Bion, 1965).

Winnicott, while taking a predominantly environmental view, always keeps in mind the importance of the coexistence of internal and external realities. when he writes in 1939 that

> to be able to tolerate all that one may find in one's inner reality is one of the great human difficulties and an important human aim is to bring into harmonious relationship one's personal inner and outer realities (…). When the cruel or destructive forces there threaten to dominate over the loving, the individual has to do something to save himself and one thing he does is to turn himself inside out, to dramatise the inner world outside, to act the destructive role himself and to bring about control by external authority.
>
> (2016, p. 69)

Even in Bion the death drive can be contemplated, but not in the original Freudian sense of tension towards the quiet, rather it remains in the Kleinian furrow of aggression and destructiveness. What is original in Bion is that this destructiveness is not only applied to the object but, in psychotics, *against the same apparatus for thinking* (a movement that he calls -k, an attack on knowledge), thus killing the love for truth that is a real, or perhaps the only, *food for mind,* and making any transformation impossible. Bion gives us an attempt to build a theory of the mind, where we see that the psychotic mind, to defend itself against pain and perception, attacks the bonds and representations, thus making therapeutic work difficult.

In the United States, lastly, the spread of intersubjectivist thought in psychoanalysis has, at least apparently, reduced interest in metapsychology and therefore in the death drive. While not denying the concept of the unconscious, for these authors, including Kohut, Stolorow, Mitchell and others, everything is based on the relationship and on the unconscious and relational, in other words, it is the result of the analyst and the patient working together. In the 1980s, a famous controversy between Kohut and Kernberg over the role of narcissism and aggression takes the place of interest in metapsychological issues. Kernberg (1976) is perhaps the North American psychoanalyst who does attempt a very important synthesis on a clinical level, between aggression, drives and object relationships. For Kernberg, aggression is an expression of the death drive, that is, it does not depend only on the environment but is also rooted within the individual. However, rather than leading to the desire for quiet as in Freud, it attacks and destroys the object.

While, therefore, for Freud and the Freudians, the presence of a death drive is underlying, and aggression and sadism are its projections on the outside, for Kernberg it is aggression that is primary.

In contemporary psychoanalysis

In recent years, many works on the death drive have been published. Here we return to Kernberg (2009). He attempts to integrate the various psychoanalytic orientations, concluding rather critically "the death drive, I suppose, is not a primary drive, but represents a significant complication of aggression (...) is central in therapeutic work with severe psychopathology, and as such is eminently useful as a concept in the clinical realm" (p. 1018). By depriving the concept of primacy as a drive, it remains clinically very useful but, in my opinion, more confusing than the Freudian concept itself.

This re-examination of the death drive also comes about thanks to Solms (2021). He delivers a careful review of Freudian theoretical positions, and seems to conclude that "there is no need to invoke the existence of a separate 'death drive' that serves the Nirvana principle; it is served by the 'life' drive and it represents the ideal state" (Solms, 2021, p. 1054). This recognition of a push to death, but which falls solely within the life drive, is very close to Laplanche's position: while he recognizes a drive to death, he does not feel the need to make it a separate drive. The mixing of biological and psychological aspects remains confused, even for Solms, while as regards the pathological manifestations that can be seen under the lens of the death drive (severe narcissism, addiction, suicidal tendencies), they can be considered "attempts to evade the reality principle, which is indeed a dangerous (and potentially fatal) thing to do. These are failings of *ego* functioning" (ibid., 2021, p. 1054).

The concept of the death drive is sometimes used to explain human violence in general, extending to abuse, domestic violence and even terrorism (Akhtar, 2017), connected with some severe psychopathological traits, such as severe personality disorders. I agree with Kirsch (2022), that although clinically useful, there is a certain theoretical inconsistency in this, as if the death drive has become an umbrella that encompasses and explains all forms of aggression. The death drive by itself does not explain the nature of aggression, which requires not only the presence of a drive universally and anthropologically present in all of us, but must meet other factors, e.g. traumatic and environmental, to express itself (for more details see Collins, 2008).

We can say, in short, that contemporary psychoanalysis shows a great interest in the reinterpretation of the death drive, dividing itself between those who find it an important or indispensable concept, and those who express doubts about its theoretical relevance, considering it basically confusing. Contemporary studies focus mainly on the clinical fallout of the death drive, in violent behaviour and in addiction, with conflicting results (Kirsch et al., 2022), on which I will return to in Chapter 8 when I focus on neuroscience's interest in the death drive.

Lacan

Lacan's thought merits a few words apart and I will also return to him when I examine masochism.

Very important in French psychoanalysis, especially around the 1960s, Lacan's thought at first influences analysts already mentioned, such as Green, Laplanche and Pontalis (the so-called first generation), who then break away from it. Lacan welcomes *Beyond the Pleasure Principle* as an "extraordinary text," "unbelievably ambiguous," (1954) which questions the very idea of progress. A revolutionary text, indeed.

Difficult to condense into a few lines and not easy to explain, Lacan's very complex thought is affected by the philosophical influences of the French climate of the time. It is particularly marked by: the French anthropologist Lévi-Strauss for the concepts of structure, family and role of the father; the Russian-born French philosopher Kojève regarding the concept of desire and the re-reading of the thoughts of Hegel; and the Swiss linguist de Saussure. Lacan calls his movement "return to Freud," to distance himself from Hartmann's Ego Psychology, widespread at the time, and essentially in favour of a thought profoundly linked to Freud's. For contemporary Lacanians, the death drive is a central concept.

Lacan, while standing well within the drive theory, does not take the biological aspect into account because for him the human being is drawn from the very start, from birth, into the symbolic order, into language. He deals with the death drive in *Seminar VII*, in his *The Ethics of Psychoanalysis (1959–1960),* because the discourse on the ethics of psychoanalysis and its management in treatment cannot be separated from that of humankind in general. For Lacan, the fact that Freud put this drive into effect can no longer be avoided, on the contrary, for him *the whole drive tends to die*, it is the drive of death. The drive is described as a push to return to the One, to the Thing (*Das Ding*), a sort of nostalgia towards the primary object that can never be realized, because the human being has undergone a "cut" at birth that has separated and immersed him in language; the subject is a "split subject" or a "barred subject" (represented as S), that is, inhabited by death the moment they enter the language. Lacan understands the extraordinary nature of *Beyond the Pleasure Principle*, the text with which Freud breaks with every hedonistic-naturalistic logic of pleasure: the eternal return of the same which in *Seminar VII* is described as a "tyranny of memory" (1994) shows the attachment of the human being to what causes pain. All pleasure, Lacan says, borders on suffering: in the soldiers' traumatic dreams, in repetition compulsion, in the symptom. When Freud describes the death drive as "the most pulsational" (*triebhafter*), for Lacan this signifies dangerous enjoyment beyond the minimum excitation, so that, in this overturned perspective, death no longer represents the inanimate, but becomes an endpoint of the enjoyment of life.

The effect of the drive is not to push towards pleasure but rather towards *enjoyment (jouissance, or jouissance mortelle)* which is anything but pleasure, it is what Freud called *the afterlife* of pleasure. Enjoyment is an excess, a more that goes beyond the limit of pleasure and towards pain (the concept, in the end, of overlapping Lust and Unlust is once again taken up). In the clinic, pleasure is within the symptom, which in fact the patient abandons with difficulty, but can correspond to the death drive to the extent that, pushing beyond normal pleasure, enjoyment becomes deadly. The whole clinic of addiction, or excess in general, in Lacanian terms is a clinic of enjoyment, of *jouissance mortelle.*

I would thus synthesize Lacan's main contribution to understanding the death drive, in his intimate understanding of what Freud meant by that "more pulsional" of the death drive: excess. Excess not only takes openly destructive forms but also, in Lacanian thought, in all those manifestations in which the subject wants to go beyond the Law of castration, that is, the limit, all those forms (as we will see in the film *The Whale,* discussed in Chapter 5) in which the subject is pushed into an enjoyment that dissolves life. Lacan, with Freud, are the great thinkers who break the Aristotelian illusion that life, through knowledge, tends towards Good. Instead, they show that the exercise of rational will is by no means sufficient to avert the risk of evil, the risk of acting against oneself, as if life hated itself. In Lacanian terms, human beings do not want to heal because they do not want to renounce the enjoyment of their Evil, even if this results in subjective suffering. Lacan therefore fully acknowledges this significant Freudian step which, with a few exceptions. including Klein, post-Freudian psychoanalysis most often reductively rejects, namely the mixture of life with death. But unlike Klein, who gives a destructive version of it as an attack on objects, Lacan places the death drive within the very darkest of human enjoyments. It should also be pointed out, however, that access to enjoyment is not an evil in itself, but only if it goes beyond the limit, beyond castration. If it is filtered by the Law, that is to say, by desire, it remains in the vital field. *Two enjoyments* may be distinguished: one that remains in the field of desire; and one, *jouissance mortelle,* that demands to go beyond it, an impossible enjoyment. The first, desire, is against the homeostasis of the principle of inertia, it is movement and restlessness; the second, however, which is a death drive, autistically tends to the One, to an enjoyment without the Other, as, indeed, addictions and certain psychotic forms are.

Notes

1 Fenichel in 1935, when he wrote *A Critique of the Death Instinct,* was still very close to Marxist thought and the possibility of an aggressive and destructive push, psychologically intrinsic to the individual, contrasted with the historical and economic determination attributed by Marxism to all. Later, he placed himself within Freudian thought.
2 By this term, Laplanche means polymorphous-perverse infantile sexuality, an enlarged, non-genital sexuality affecting all human life.
3 The symposium's papers and dialogues were summarized in part by Rabain in a special issue of the Revue française de psychanalyse in 1989.

Chapter 4

How is the "silent" drive expressed? Masochism's dangerous derivative

Defining masochism: is there more than one masochism?

I have dedicated a chapter to masochism, following the Freudian approach. Indeed, Freud devoted an essay to masochism in 1924, *The Economic Problem of Masochism*. The complex phenomenon of masochism can be approached from different angles; in fact, philosophers have dealt with it. But it was Freud who ventured a psychoanalytic understanding and a systemization of it. The term has eased its way into common usage. When most people think of masochism, they think of a strange phenomenon whereby the individual experiences pleasure in pain, derives pleasure from hurting, physically or psychologically, becoming damaged in various ways even to their complete ruin, all the while seeking, consciously or unconsciously, this pleasure. Given that the term has entered popular use, then evidently we all know one way or another what we mean when we talk about masochism, and perhaps no one is completely immune to it.

We can imagine a spectrum, ranging from the most pathological (such as masochistic perversion or severe self-destructive behaviour) to the most nuanced or sporadic situations in a person's life. There are masochistic "characters," in which all personality style is set in this sense and who, as characters, tend not to change (Reich, 1933; McWilliams, 1994), just as masochism can represent a contingency in life, where even different personalities can, for some internal or external reason, temporarily take on masochistic traits (for example, during bereavement or within a sadomasochistic pathological relationship). Lastly, we know that masochistic acts are not uncommon in children and adolescents. As we can see, this is an extremely complex

DOI: 10.4324/9781003474678-5

landscape, so much so that, in my opinion, the designation *not one but many masochisms* is justified.

Why does Freud wait four years to deal specifically with masochism if it is a derivative of the death drive? And how does masochism relate to sadism, the seemingly opposite phenomenon with which it is commonly linked?

At 12 pages, his essay is rather short yet very complex, as Freud attempts to establish masochism within the subject, as a derivation of the death drives that are innate in the individual and that, as we have seen, can cancel the pleasure principle. We read in Freud:

> Moral masochism becomes a classical piece of evidence for the existence of *fusion of instinct.* Its danger lies in the fact that *it originates from the death instinct* and corresponds to the *part of that instinct which has escaped being turned outwards* as an instinct of destruction. But since, on the other hand, it has the significance of an erotic component, even the subject's destruction of himself cannot take place without libidinal satisfaction.
>
> (1924, p. 170, my italics)

This quote, I believe, contains Freud's real definition of masochism: masochism is the fruit of the pulsional mixture between the life and death drives, it emanates from that part of the death drive that remains inside the organism, which does not turn outwards into sadism and is extraordinarily dangerous because, if it is accompanied by an unconscious pleasure, it leads an individual to self-destruction. Masochism is, therefore, inherent in human beings from birth. Part of our drive baggage, it is represented by that share of the initial death drive that remains, for various reasons, within the organism.

At this point we need to take a step back. At first, masochism represents only a sexual perversion, cited by Freud in *Three Essays on the Theory of Sexuality* (1905). The term comes from the Austrian writer Leopold von Sacher-Masoch, author of the novella *Venus in Furs*,[1] which was inspired by his own life, and of a diary in which he writes of his masochistic perversion deriving from a childhood scene that remained fixed in his memory: spying on his fur-clad aunt as she whipped her lover. When the child was discovered, he was beaten, with this indelible scene (we don't know if this was real, phantasy or a screen memory[2]) remaining in his mind and determining his entire sexual life, marked by a desire to be beaten by a woman. The first clinician to observe this phenomenon was the German psychiatrist Krafft-Ebing, whose 1886 *Psychopathia Sexualis* is one of the first books about sexual pathology; it has therefore always existed.

The interest in masochism, which Freud calls an "enigma," goes far beyond a bizarre sexual perversion, which can be present in various degrees. It is an increasingly important theme for Freud because it is linked to the death drive and to the potential that an individual has to self-destruct.

The Freudian path

When it comes to masochism, Freud is most interested in it as a sexual perversion, often but not necessarily combined with the counterpart of sadism.[3] In *Three Essays on the Theory of Sexuality* (1905), he places masochism in the sadism-masochism couple, where a masochist always corresponds to a sadist, depending on whether the passive or active aspect is acted out, and the two roles can be reversed. Sexual perversion remains unchanged over time, but Freud's interest extends far beyond the confines of perversion, questioning the role of passivity and the search for pain in the human being, which represents an unresolved paradox. Humans can feel pleasure in pain because, as we have seen in the previous chapter, pleasure and sorrow are not so distinguishable (*Lust-Unlust*) and masochistic pleasure, for example in perversion, is the result of a "libidinal co-excitation" (Freud, 1924), in which pain and pleasure are closely linked, in fact inseparable, and therefore indistinguishable. In *The Economic Problem of Masochism* in 1924, Freud goes back almost 20 years, to *Three Essays on the Theory of Sexuality*, where he had written:

> In the case of a great number of internal processes sexual excitation arises as a concomitant effect, as soon as the intensity of those processes passes beyond certain quantitative limits (…). In accordance with this, the excitation of pain and unpleasure would be bound to have the same result, too. The occurrence of such a libidinal sympathetic excitation when there is a tension due to pain and unpleasure would be an infantile physiological mechanism which ceases later on (…) in any case it would provide the physiological foundation on which the psychical structure of erotogenic masochism would afterwards be erected.

> (1924, p. 163, vol. 19)

Initially Freud believes that sadism precedes masochism, that is, that masochism is actually a sadism reflected on one's own person (1915). He changes his mind later on, affirming *masochism as primary* to sadism (1924). This is a very important step, not only for its metapsychological construction, but for the very vision it provides of humankind. We come into the world in a *masochistic* position, in the sense of a *primary passivity* that during our lifetime may be avoided but may also be libidinalized, to become again a source of pleasure – a masochistic pleasure, a passive pleasure.

Another significant step comes in 1919 in the form of the essay *A Child Is Being Beaten: A Contribution to the Study of the Origin of Sexual Perversions*. Here, Freud investigates the masochistic phantasies of some of his patients, childhood phantasies that occur with unusual frequency. A child in the Oedipal phase associates great pleasure with the beatings he receives from his father. Freud breaks the scene down into several stages. In the first, the father beats another child, for example a brother, a hated child (the phantasy up to now is not masochistic). The scene evolves and is turned *on the subject's person: "I am beaten by my father."* This second part is the most important one because it is where phantasy becomes masochistic and entails intense pleasure. A masochistic phantasy has been formed in the boy, or more often the girl, and will remain for a lifetime inside the subject. This intense incestuous love is destined to be repressed, leaving as a legacy *the sense of Oedipal guilt* that we often find in the adult patient, linked to early, strongly eroticized phantasies. It should be made clear that here Freud considers the object of incestuous love, for both male and female, to be always the father, within the "negative" Oedipal complex for the boy (who in this case would passively love the father) and the "positive" Oedipal complex for the girl. The unconscious equation is *my father loves me/my father beats me*. I believe that it is possible that this kind of phantasy could contribute to certain cases of so-called female masochism, all those cases that also make the news in which women suffer but do not rebel against their torturers. The phenomenon is complex and controversial, and I will address it separately.

Another outcome of this phantasy is *identification with the aggressor*, a defence mechanism observed by Anna Freud in 1936. In this case, those who have been mistreated, rather than rebelling, unconsciously identify with the aggressor by becoming themselves an aggressor towards other people or internally towards themselves. We observe this phenomenon in abusive families, where it is not uncommon for children who have been abused to become violent parents; or, if everything happens in the internal world, the person who has been abused may become abusive towards themselves, that is to say, they may develop masochistic behaviour or seek only damaging bonds that cause suffering (Eigen, 2001). Another group-level reflection of this phenomenon is the so-called Stockholm syndrome, which happens when people who have been kidnapped become attached to, or even fall in love with, their captors.[4] Similar situations of group regressions are observed in certain fanatical religious sects whose members submit completely to their leader to the point of losing their lives. In children, identification with the attacker can be a necessary survival mechanism if they depend on the attacking adult, while in cases of Stockholm syndrome it is possible that the mechanism is initially similarly linked to survival only to then become a masochistic fixation to the trauma.

All these phenomena, if read in the key of masochism, make clear just how complex the psychopathology of trauma is, which is perhaps talked about all too freely nowadays. Those who suffer oppression in an intimate relationship, one of caring, can, in turn, develop a libidinal attachment that leverages precisely the unconscious masochistic setting.

The economic problem of masochism

This is how Freud opens *The Economic Problem of Masochism*, his essay on masochism:

> The existence of a masochistic trend in the instinctual life of human beings may justly be described as *mysterious* from the economic point of view. For if mental processes are governed by the pleasure principle in such a way that their first aim is the avoidance of unpleasure and the obtaining of pleasure, masochism is incomprehensible. If pain and unpleasure can be not simply warnings but actually *aims*, the pleasure principle is paralyzed – it is as though the watchman over our mental life were put out of action by a drug.
> (Freud, 1924, p. 153)

Masochism *mysterious* because it does not tally with the pleasure principle, for in masochism the individual seeks unpleasure and pain; pain is no longer a warning but an end to be pursued, and by paralysing the pleasure principle, life may be endangered. In this essay Freud seems to attempt to return the enigmatic masochism to a *Lust* economy, that is, to the rule of the pleasure principle. Given that two years earlier he admits that not everything in the psyche tends to pleasure, this may seem like a step backwards, but that is not the case: until the end, Freud always gives *Lust* dominion, and the hereafter of *Lustprinzip* is always a limit, a margin, something that extends beyond. In short, Freud never renounces his own paradigm based on the *pleasure principle*: what exceeds it will emerge as a limit or paradox of pleasure, not as something that will trample over it completely, break it, defeat it. Freud always holds the pleasure principle as his fundamental interpretative rule: the beyond – Eros and Thanatos – always appears huddled between the lines. But we have seen *Lust*'s ambiguity; masochism poses a problem.

Here is an example. If I pass a place where there is fire and I burn myself, I will feel an intense pain that will make me move away from that dangerous source: pain is a warning to preserve life (both for human beings and animals). But it may also be that despite feeling pain from the fire, or *in order to feel that pain*, I do not protect myself by moving away, but I return to that pain-inducing source. It is precisely this second paradoxical and counterintuitive mechanism that happens only in human beings. Only we choose to suffer, to harm ourselves, to seek pleasure in pain sometimes or for completely unconscious reasons. We could say that, by virtue of the death drive and the resulting masochism, a person's life in his own hands is in danger.

Given this premise, Freud identifies three types of masochism: (1) primary or erogenous masochism; (2) feminine masochism and; (3) moral masochism. When we use the word "masochism" we actually mean moral masochism, which may also be called "secondary masochism."

Primary masochism, from which the other two derive, is the darkest of all. Its foundation must be sought out in biological factors. Freud defines it as, "…evidence of, and a remainder from, the phase of development in which the coalescence, which is so important for life, between the death instinct and Eros took place" (1924, p. 164). It represents that part that is not extroflected as sadism but remains in the organism. Sadism has become secondary, it is only a necessary extroflection of a quota of the death drive that would otherwise destroy the whole organism.[5] This type of masochism is also called erogenous because it is thanks to the link with Eros that life within the organism can affirm itself. Laplanche calls it "originary" (2000) and Lacan "fundamental" (1962–1963).

We can find the expression of too weak primary erogenous masochism, for example, in neonatal marasmus or in hospitalism, the term Réne Spitz (1945) introduces on the heels of the Second World War. The Austrian-American psychoanalyst extensively studied children abandoned in orphanages, fed regularly but bereft of interpersonal contact, especially with the mother. Despite being fed, many of these children let themselves die of starvation, as if, according to this metapsychological reading, maternal absence caused drive de-fusion, with the lack of a necessary object to libidinally bind the death drive left it free to harm.[6] Lest we think these are phenomena belonging to the past, we should remind ourselves that even today many children suffer from this condition, for example, due to war.

Feminine masochism is the simplest of the three forms, according to Freud. He observes it in phantasies of masochistic and often impotent men, whose desire was to be "gagged, bound, painfully beaten, whipped, in some way maltreated, forced into unconditional obedience, dirtied and debased" (1924, p. 162).

Feminine masochism corresponds to the masochistic perversion of Sacher-Masoch, which can be performed or only fantasized or, as is often seen with patients in analysis, present in dreams and phantasies (including of heterosexual patients).

The term has lent itself to much misunderstanding and been confused, especially in the post-Freud period, with female masochism (Deutsch, 1945). This conflation is partly due to the fact that the English language, through which Freud is known worldwide, uses the term "feminine" for both meanings, namely to convey a passive sense and second as an adjective of the noun "female." In my own research in Italian[7] I have been able to separate the two terms for "feminine" (in English there is only one word) into "femmineo" and "femininile," clarifying what I see as a critical misunderstanding of which I will speak later.

Moral masochism is the most important of the three forms, that is, masochism as commonly understood outside of perversion. Here masochism is, so to speak, de-erotized: *what matters is the suffering itself*, not where it comes from. The most common type of masochism is also the most difficult to treat or even to recognize. This is particularly dangerous in analysis because it is the cause of strong *negative therapeutic reactions*, that is, the patient unconsciously opposes healing to satisfy their unconscious guilt and the need for punishment that ensues. Freud writes:

> The satisfaction of this unconscious sense of guilt is perhaps the most powerful bastion in the subject's (usually composite) gain from illness (...) The suffering entailed by neuroses is precisely the factor that makes them valuable to the masochistic trend.
>
> (1924, p. 166)

I believe that every clinician has come up against this painful phenomenon more than once in their work. Usually what happens is that the patient has improved and then unexpectedly things get worse, everything seems to have gone back to the start, or therapy is abandoned. Being sick, physically or mentally, satisfies the severe unconscious feeling of guilt, caused by a pathological sadistic Super-Ego. Let us bear in mind that in 1924 the second Freudian topography has already appeared, structuring the tripartition of the psychic apparatus in Id, Ego and Super-Ego (*The Ego and the Id*, 1923). Although there is apparently no sexual pleasure, the moral masochist seems to enjoy suffering as if it were sexual pleasure, and always proffers the other cheek when any hitting is to be done. Freud calls this masochism "moral" not because the person is moral or moralistic, on the contrary, but because of the connection with the Super-Ego, which is the ethical component of the personality and provides the moral standards by which the Ego operates. This masochism is the most dangerous of all, even when unostentatious, as every clinician knows. The danger of moral masochism lies in the fact that Eros, the libido, is no longer present, so the subject can "enjoy" pure unhappiness as if it were sexual satisfaction, without the contribution of the Other, because the sado-masochistic pair is formed within the individual: sadistic Super-Ego versus masochistic Ego. This can lead, in the extreme, to melancholia or, in transference, to certain tenacious negative therapeutic reactions.

A notable example of moral masochism in a highly successful man was Dostoevsky, to whom Freud dedicates the essay *Dostoevsky and Parricide* (1927). Suffering from epilepsy, the great writer recovers only when he is deported to Siberia, that is, when he suffers a punishment and therefore an atonement for his unconscious guilt (he gambles to excess and loses a lot of money). Many of his characters are equally persecuted by guilt and masochism, which can lead them, as in *Crime and Punishment,* to become *Criminals from a Sense of Guilt* (Freud, 1916): crime is committed in order to be punished.

On those wrecked by success

The short paper just mentioned, *Criminals from a Sense of Guilt,* together with the interesting *On Those Wrecked by Success,* form part of the 1916 essay *Some Character-Types Met within Psycho-Analytic Work,* replete with intuition to be found again in his 1924 work. Here Freud describes the kind of people we have all certainly met in the clinic and in life, who become ill when they get what they said they desired, or who unconsciously fail at something they care about and appear "… as though they were not able to tolerate their happiness" (Freud, 1916, p. 157).

What is there to say about this strange phenomenon? Success, in fact, is not easy to bear. It may be an Oedipal success, that is, the realization of the phantasy that with our success we kill our parents,[8] or it may be a success that triggers the anguish of having to grow and evolve in life, as is the case with students who get stuck at the hurdle of end-of-degree exams or graduation. Lastly, success may not be endured by a masochistic personality who draws narcissistic reinforcement from feeling the victim. I believe that even some interruptions in analysis may be related to the fear that the treatment will succeed and expose the patient to changes that he does not want to face.

The case of F.: self-punishment

F. comes to seek my help, at the age of about 30, because he has strange somatizations. He says he is completely blocked by gastric pain, abdominal swelling and above all an extreme fatigue that prevents him from carrying out normal activities. No doctor or gastroenterologist has identified which illness afflicts him. F. is not convinced that the root is psychological and stubbornly seeks a physical ailment.

F. is a brilliant young man who, until a few months earlier, was studying to become a theatre actor and was about to be called on to tour by a director, his teacher, who he holds in high esteem. Theatre is his passion. He has devoted years of study to it but now, because of these stomach problems and fatigue, he has given it up. So F. does nothing. He no longer studies nor does he work. Later he will dial down to rather modest jobs. To his great regret, he will never go back to theatre.

A rather peculiar family picture emerges from his history. F. is very attached to his brother who is four years older than him and who lives in isolation. He is possibly psychotic with deeply paranoid ideas. He is stuck in his studies due to his mental disorder. The mother, who will die during our analysis, raised the two boys with the conscious and unconscious mandate to *be equal*, neither of them was to have more or less, as if in the maternal phantasy the two boys were not separate and could not differentiate themselves, or there was only room for one. Analytical work will show how F. punished himself masochistically, through this incurable somatization, at a time when he was about to achieve a success that in his phantasy corresponded to doing away with his brother.

One dream is clear: F. is driving a car and he runs over a disabled person. With his individualistic conduct (driving the car), moving on in life, he kills someone perceived as a disabled person. He associates this disabled person with his brother. Because he cannot be different, he becomes "disabled" too.

Over time, although his professional situation improves with analysis, F. does not return to the theatre. From time to time his strange physical symptoms flare up again, as if a certain price to pay always remains (metapsychologically, a certain erotization of the organ of a masochistic order).

Mrs. B. and the open book

When analysis begins, Mrs. B. is a very unhappy woman. She has just managed to divorce from a narcissistic-sadistic man with whom she had been very much in love. In the first few years of analysis, she describes in detail the harassment and humiliation to which he subjected her. He told her that she was never beautiful enough, either too thin or too fat, never good enough, always imperfect and incapable. In their sex life, he imposed strict rituals that she had to undergo without any pleasure, while he was impotent. In everyday life, Mrs. B. is an efficient bank clerk. Everyone relies on her because she is the most precise, the last to leave the office, the most rigorous (like the Russian writer, moral masochists can be successful people, thanks to their spirit of sacrifice). Nothing escapes her Super-Ego! In family life it is she who cares for the elderly, sick father and performs all the tasks, it is she who thinks of everything. It is not uncommon, as I have noted in several women with masochistic behaviours, for accidents to occur, such as falls in the house or sudden fleeting symptoms that she stoically endures (but by bringing the injured body to the analyst, the patient carries a tale of Self that she wants to be read, understood and interpreted).

Lengthy analytical work will highlight in Mrs. B's childhood the relationship with a hostile and depressed mother who greatly neglected her, but to whom the child (the last of three siblings and "born by mistake") tried to make herself useful by physically caring for her. In adult life she transfers her capacity for caring to her husband, relatives, friends, both in the hope of being loved and to gain a sense of identity and a narcissistic return. The masochistic submission to her husband allowed her to "keep him tied to herself" but also gave her identity, and in suffering Mrs. B. felt she existed. As with F., it takes time for this patient to recognize her unconscious contribution to the way her life is going to ruin, to take responsibility and not feel a victim of tragic destiny. This short dream in Mrs. B.'s second year of analysis proves important: "*I left the book open.*"

She associates that she was in the house where she was with her husband and that the book was a diary that should have been closed, re-served. *The open book* becomes for us, in the language of the analytic couple, the metaphor of her not being protected, of her exposing her-self in the hope of receiving something. The image's sexual reference is also evident. During her analytical work, Mrs. B. will slowly learn to put up fences, protect herself and feel like someone even without necessarily getting hurt.

The problem of "feminine" masochism

In the wake of Mrs. B.'s case, and the many patients I have seen in similar situations, I propose a reflection on a thorny and controversial issue about which I believe psychoanalysis should attempt some hy-potheses. It is not uncommon to hear in the media about women who do not rebel against violent partners, who even return to them when they have a chance to separate, in short, who generally make them-selves vulnerable. Can we therefore speak of a masochism typical of women, even today when a certain level of equality has been achieved in the field of work and money? The women I am talking about, such as Mrs. B., are, in fact, educated and in a sound economic position and would have every means to avoid being humiliated.

To return to Freud and his definition of "feminine" masochism, as I said before, I believe that Freud has no intention of attributing masochism to a gender, but by "feminine," on the contrary, he means *passive* phantasies which, paradoxically, are observed in male patients but can appear in both men and women. While the Italian language allows for this subtle distinction between "femmineo" and "femminile," using the English word "feminine" for both may have lent itself to misunderstanding and to accusations, especially by feminist psychoanalysts, directed at Freud.

My hypothesis is that masochism, or masochisms, is a vast archipelago where, by virtue of the primary masochism present in all of us, which bases life in passivity, this position can be invested in during a human being's life for various reasons: to experience enjoyment, to feel alive and animated, to take a position in relation to the Other.

From my clinical experience, and from observing life and society, the *position* (and not a structure) – which women consciously and not infrequently assume of "self-objectification" and, as Lacanian authors say, of being a waste-object (Fiumanò, 2016), that is to identify oneself, like Cinderella, with something that has no value and can be thrown away – allows certain women with a very fragile narcissistic setting to be something to someone, to *become subjects* for another, we might say "by proxy." Better to be a mistreated subject, to be the woman "of" someone, than to be no one. There is never erotic pleasure in this position because it is not perversion in the strict sense which, as is known, is almost exclusively male. By "position" (assumed by the woman) I mean that the woman is not structurally masochistic but becomes *"un semblant"* (Lacan, 1972–1973): she "pretends," she plays at femininity in order to enter the male phantasy, that is to say, to be accepted by the man as the object of his desire. It is the same concept that the British Kleinian psychoanalyst Joan Riviere, who is very distant from Lacan, takes up when she speaks of "womanliness as a masquerade" (1929). But this is a dangerous road to tread, with masochistic stumbling blocks, excesses and vacillation towards a truly masochistic position lurking just around the corner if the woman goes too far in this position, one she believes guarantees her a place in her man. We have also seen the incestuous phantasy described in *A Child Being Beaten*, which can contribute to this eroticization of pain in some women, creating confusion between suffering and being loved.

"How much *do you value my desire?*" is an eternal lovers' question. But the supposed value, for example, of *feminine masochism*, of how it is expressed, should be put within the context of a troublesome question. It is part of a dialogue that in many cases can be defined as a fantasy of male desire (Lacan, 1964). When Lacan replies to American and British psychoanalysts and to Freud's colleague, the Polish-American psychoanalyst Helene Deutsch, who instead was convinced of passivity and masochism in women, he remarks that feminine masochism "cannot be considered to be simply a homonym for 'passivity'." He then poses the question: "Can we rely on what masochistic perversion owes to male invention and conclude that female masochism is a fantasy of male desire?" He adds: "In any case, I will denounce the irresponsible mental retardation that claims to deduce fantasies of the breaking of corporal boundaries" (Lacan, 2006, p. 615). Lacan further specifies that "the masculine ideal and the feminine ideal are represented in the psyche by something other than this activity/passivity opposition" (Lacan, 1977, pp. 192–193). When Lacan specifies that masochism is a fantasy of male desire, this assumes that it is only a fantasy. The passage to the masochistic act is obviously no longer a fantasy but a sexual assault or a perverse act.

In other words, the so-called masochism that is ascribed to women would in fact be a male fantasy. In my experience, analytical work can successfully help female patients to free themselves from the role of victim by re-establishing a vital narcissism, a "minimum necessary narcissism" (Bolognini, 2008), an ability to self-confirm which has been hampered by the many traumas suffered during development (Mrs. B. had also suffered childhood abuse by a shopkeeper against which, as a child, she had not rebelled). It is in my experience that if a woman comes to analysis in these cases, there is already an awareness and the treatment can proceed with some success.

Masochism and narcissism: after Freud

In the post-Freud period, the main insights into masochism come from French authors in both psychoanalytic and philosophical areas (Sartre, 1943; Deleuze, 1967) because masochism is a universal phenomenon that concerns human nature and is not confined to the clinic.

Among the post-Freudian contributions, I mention the work of one of Freud's first students, Theodor Reik (1941), still relevant today, on the masochistic character, its expressions and inclinations, and the intuition, already existing in Freud, that often the masochist is a subject who *wants,* or insists, that his suffering is seen and displayed.

As for Lacan, we have seen that he considers the death drive as central, and the same applies to masochism, which, in fact, he calls "fundamental." The masochist, he writes, is "*le vrai maître*" (1964) (the real master); it is he who guides the sadomasochistic game, while the sadist's pleasure derives from identification with the masochist. In the clinic, we sometimes see how the two roles are easily reversed and, in fact, the games end when it is "the victim" who moves away (as in the case of Mrs. B.). The change of role can also take place within the same person, as with Sacher-Masoch, who upon the death of his beloved wife fell into deep depression, to then become rather sadistic with a family he took into service.

Reik's work contains the intuition that will be developed by Robert Stolorow, who belongs to the Self Psychology group, which I consider to be one of the most important post-Freudian contributions, namely that masochism and narcissism, seemingly distant, actually go together: masochism represents, as the clinic well shows, a paradoxical and important narcissistic reinforcement.

To complete the understanding of masochism, I consider indispensable reading Stolorow's *The Narcissistic Function of Masochism (and Sadism)*, which appeared in the *International Journal of Psychoanalysis* in 1975. He writes that in masochistic perversion the masochist may need the feeling of acute pain to *strengthen their feeling of having a cohesive self*, before risking the threat of self-loss due to sexual intimacy. Stolorow argues that the patient can seek a grotesque feeling of pain to restore the boundary of the Self and *rebuild a narcissistic integrity* when their self-representation is threatened. He asserts that self-aggression is a peculiar human response to self-offence and serves the individual's effort to repair the damaged self-representation. Aggression is at the service of psychic survival and in the treatment of the masochist it follows that an analysis of the victim (narcissistic vulnerability) takes priority over the analysis of disturbing behaviour (hostile aggression) (1979).

This valuable contribution helps to understand, as in the case of Mrs. B. and many other patients, that masochism is a *strategy* that the patient puts in place to restore a fragmented, fragile or absent sense of self. Sometimes, in order to obtain a secondary gain, we think of the child who "feels sick" to avoid going to school and to stay with his mother, as my patient David used to do as a child, to escape the pain and fatigue of school. He lost many months of school due to various "illnesses:" instead of being a bullied child in class, he became a small child cared for by his parents at home. This secondary gain inevitably grows stronger over time because it involves a narcissistic gain.

Stolorow offers us an important suggestion for our clinical work, namely to give precedence to work on the narcissistic structure, because it is useless and even counterproductive at the beginning to highlight unconscious aggression. His observations are shared by other authors of the North American school (Cooper et al., 1988), and represent an evolution not only of Freud's thought, but also of Ferenczi (1932), Brenner (1959) and Reik (1941). On the metapsychological level, there is also agreement with Freud, in the sense that in both narcissism and masochism, all libido focuses on the Ego, although paradoxically causing pain.

At the extreme of this dynamic we can see the phenomenon of sacrifice, for example, for religious or political reasons, where the "victim," who usually dies happy, offers their body to an excruciatingly painful death in exchange for the deep narcissistic gratification of being loved by God or of contributing to an important cause. On the other hand, however, masochism and narcissism, if they reinforce each other in excess, can form a deadly cocktail, as we see in certain stubborn negative therapeutic reactions.

I would conclude these reflections on masochism, certainly neither exhaustive nor complete, with these words of Michel de M'Uzan:

> In order to manage the tensions that come from both the external and the internal pulsional world, everyone has some 'tools' from which they 'choose,' according to the circumstances, according to the intensity of the forces at play (and number), the most suitable. Ideally, we can choose the mental pathway more often, including neurotic forms. But it may happen that this pathway is insufficient, and it is then that, remaining in the mental register, one can 'opt' for the psychotic thread. (…) This may be a better solution, if any, than a somatic disease. (…) In truth, the allusion of a choice is evidently provocative because this happens without the subject's knowledge. That being the case it is apparent that *I am bringing perverse erogenous masochism into the framework of the management tools* (of excess).
>
> (2000, p. 141, translated for this edition, my italics)

To sum up, it is impossible to encapsulate in a handful of pages the enormous phenomenon of masochism, a transclinical and transcultural phenomenon which can affect every psychic structure (depressive, hysterical, obsessive) and settle inside a character or be seen as a contingency or even an "instrument," at certain moments in life. It can manifest itself in sexuality as a perversion or just a phantasy, representing a childhood *fixation* that characterizes the subject's life. It can give rise to destiny neuroses and self-boycotts, or express itself in the body with somatic diseases to satisfy the need for punishment. Clinically speaking, moral masochism can block analysis in the form of negative therapeutic reactions, thwart success in treatment and, even then, self-destruction brings the subject omnipotent narcissistic pleasure. We have also seen how masochism has a useful and necessary aspect for life.

As an expression of the death drive, therefore, it is only fatal when it exceeds, when it is detached from Eros.

Only by understanding masochism within the Lust/Unlust dialectic that is aware of the ambiguous nature of human pleasure, can we attempt a metapsychological understanding of this truly enigmatic phenomenon.

Notes

1 Director Roman Polanski made a film based on the novella in 2013.
2 Also called cover memory or replacement memory, the American Psychological Association describes it as the memory of a childhood experience, very often trivial, that unconsciously conceals, screens out or is a conflation of a more significant and possibly traumatic associated experience.
3 There are also those who have argued, such as French philosopher Deleuze (1967), that masochism is a phenomenon in its own right and, as such, completely independent of sadism.
4 The syndrome's name comes from a kidnapping case in Stockholm in 1973, when a paroled convict attempted to rob the Kreditbanken and held three women and one man hostage for six days. When they were freed, the hostages seemed to fear the police more than the robber to whom they were grateful and to whom they had become extraordinarily attached.
5 In Kleinian theorization, by contrast, it is the projection, that is sadism, which is primitive, and consideration of masochism is of no interest.
6 I am aware that there are many other interpretations of the phenomenon, such as the lack of holding and maternal mirroring (Winnicott, 1965); of reverie (Bion, 1962); of self-object (Kahut, 1971, 1977). However, even a greater focus on the role of the object does not, in my view, contradict the parallel role of drive de-fusion: it is precisely the lack of the primary object that causes de-fusion and therefore the death drive.
7 R. Valdrè (2020): *Sul masochismo. L'Enigma della Psicoanalisi*. Riflessioni nella teoria, nella clinica, nell'arte (Celid, Turin, translated for this edition)
8 Freud speaks of this feeling in *A Disturbance of Memory on the Acropolis* (1936).

Chapter 5

Clinical and artistic examples of the death drive in the individual and in social groups

Death drive and masochism in cinema: Lars von Trier

All art, especially contemporary art, is imbued with masochism and the death drive. That being the case, I have selected for this chapter only a few well-known artists who I deem particularly significant.

"Everything that is masochistic in the film is me."

The Danish film director Lars von Trier declared this in a 2014 Venice Film Festival interview. Like many artists, he transferred his emotional life, his depressive suffering (which he faced for years with alcohol, psychiatric care and psychotherapy), to his cinema. Highly creative, he is one of the few contemporary filmmakers to have co-founded an avant-garde movement, Dogma 95. After years of great success and recognition at major film festivals, his star has almost disappeared. What could have happened? I believe that the director is among *Those Wrecked By Success* (Freud, 1916): at the height of his fame, at a press conference before the premiere of his film *Melancholia* at the 2011 Cannes Film Festival, he praised Nazism. He immediately issued a formal apology but the festival banned him, his image took a hit and he had difficulties distributing the film. As a good masochist, the director was damaged at his luckiest moment.

His work, however, is a truly magnificent manifesto of the intimate exploration of the death drive and masochism. This is particularly so of his early films that made up *The Golden Heart Trilogy*, namely *Breaking the Waves* (1996), *The Idiots* (1998) and *Dancer in the Dark* (2000).

All three, feature an extremely good, generous, female protagonist with a *heart of gold*, who ends up dying or being killed for her altruism, a sacrifice pushed so much to the extreme that it constitutes true

DOI: 10.4324/9781003474678-6

masochism. Anna Freud called this attitude altruistic surrender (1936), having observed it in female patients who renounced their sexuality in adulthood to devote themselves to good works and charity. These were modest and unassuming women who wished nothing for themselves. Analysis showed that they had removed their strong sexual desires, unacceptable to the severe super-Ego, and were allowed to live them only by projecting them onto others.

Let us consider the first of the films of *The Golden Heart Trilogy*, the most well-known and fascinating, *Breaking the Waves.*

In a small, bigoted Calvinist community in the Scottish Highlands, young Bess, a good and naive girl, falls madly in love with Jan, a charming man who works on oil rigs in the stormy sea to which the title refers. Bess is strange. No one loves her. Her mother is hard and strict. Her fellow villagers think she is a little crazy. Only with Jan does she experience the intoxication of love and feels like a person for the first time. But soon after disaster hits. A work accident leaves Jan paralysed, and therefore sexually impotent. Bess doesn't care about Jan's condition, she loves him anyway, she will always love him and she spends her days at his hospital bedside. Initially he tries to push her away, but then he comes up with another idea: if she makes love with other men, then she could tell him about it and, through her words, he could relive their love as if they were together. The plan is insane and dangerous, and the few people who care about her (a doctor and her cousin) try to dissuade her. But Bess wants to please her Jan. She trades her own needs for humiliation and danger. She begins a degrading series of sexual encounters with unknown men, is even further distanced from her mother and the villagers and ends up being killed, having been violently raped. After her death, Jan is "reborn," he starts walking again, as if Bess' sacrifice had given him his life back. Bess gets herself killed for him, vilified and humiliated by everyone.

In death, Bess has a smile on her face: without him she could not have lived, but *for* him she becomes a heroine and her sacrifice saves him from sickness and death. Her final smile indicates the *deep-seated narcissistic reward of masochistic endeavour*; a little girl who was a no one has now been able to give life back to her love, thanks to her crazed will. Bess *has become an object for the other*, as Lacan wrote about the masochist (1964).

The film is a powerful artistic expression – spiced up with some magical realism – of what we have seen in the case of F., the young man who unconsciously sacrifices himself so as not to differentiate himself from his brother, which to him would have represented murder and is the cause of intolerable guilt. In the case of F., indeed, the betrayal is twofold because it concerns both maternal desire and the brother.

The protagonists of the other two films of the trilogy, Karen and Selma, also sacrifice themselves completely for their object of love, in an unequivocal despoiling and mortification of themselves without ever complaining, backtracking, or showing resentment. As Reik (1941) notes, such women do not; on the contrary there is a *demonstrativeness* in their masochistic action, as if they are shouting to the world, "Hey, look at me!" Subjects at last, such conduct, which brings them to death smiling like saints of past centuries, cannot happen without pleasure.[1] But we have seen that it is a pleasure which *does not respond to the pleasure principle*: thanks to *libidinal coexcitation* (Freud, 1924), it is a pleasure that unites with pain and is confused with pain. It is *the beyond of pleasure*, the death drive, the *jouissance.*

Some suicides centre around such sacrificial fantasies, for example, in certain religious sects or with teenagers who become followers of a group. Let's look at a very topical such case.

The Blue Whale Challenge: the death drive in teenagers

A suicide game called the Blue Whale Challenge is believed to have appeared on social media[2] in 2016. Little is known about it. The name derives from an unexplained phenomenon whereby whales and other cetaceans go to die on beaches, that is, they go to a place where they cannot survive: the act would seem like suicide. In the game, which appears to have originated in Russia, an administrator gives the rules to teens, who are to perform 50 increasingly complex tasks, the last of which is to kill themselves. As happens with adolescents, the phenomenon becomes emulative. Such a copycat game wouldn't be possible with just one person. The deciding factor is the *group* which, hidden and protected in the virtual world, in the leader finds someone with whom to identify, someone who lays down rules and says what to do, so that the final task – suicide – turns into a victory.

Suicide is the second leading cause of death in adolescents after accidents, which are often masked suicides. The causes of adolescent suicide are deeply complex. Unhappy, withdrawn kids, living in the virtual world with no connection to reality, unable to face the tasks of the evolutionary process of individuation, find in the fatal sacrifice of the game, and probably in the mere fact of belonging to a collective contest, greater cohesion of a fragile and inconsistent Self, as we saw earlier in Stolorow's writings. The administrator, who gives the orders and rules, is a stand-in for a father, who, in the lives of many contemporary adolescents, is often absent, physically or in function.

The group: mass psychology

The Blue Whale Challenge and many other social-media phenomena like it are only possible in a group. So what happens in groups? The psychoanalytic study of groups arose from another fundamental Freudian essay, *Group Psychology and the Analysis of the Ego* (1921). Just a year after *Beyond the Pleasure Principle*, Freud clearly has in mind the idea of a death drive within the individual, which will therefore inevitably also be active in groups. Indeed, because of some of the phenomena described in this essay, the death drive is even easier to activate in groups and masses.

In short, in *Group Psychology and the Analysis of the Ego* (an essay that was later considered to be almost prophetic about the advent of Nazism), Freud questions what united groups and large groups such as the masses. He proceeds with an initial careful examination of literature, which had already identified the phenomena of suggestion, critical sense decay and group hypnosis. The individual, when in a large group, can lose critical sense, loosen super-Egoic inhibitions and commit acts of violence against others or against themselves that an isolated individual would not perform. Freud, however, is not content with these exact preconditions. He looks for the psychoanalytic elements in all of this, identifying two essential factors: the libidinal bond between members and the absolute need for a leader, who will never be challenged as long as the mass exists. On this leader is projected the Ego Ideal of each group member, so that the leader becomes perfect, without defects. He represents the ideal that each one would want to be, as well as an imaginary father. The libidinal bond between the members explains the *love*, the sense of indissoluble union, that exists between the members of a mass (Freud gives the Church and the Army as examples of two great masses organized and stable over time), even if they hardly know each other.

The masses can accomplish great things, such as revolutions, but they can also become ferocious and unquestioning, as happened with Nazism and similar phenomena, for example, during wars and dictatorships. Active in the individual, the life and death drives are also at play in groups. Masochism, precisely because of the phenomena described by Freud in this essay, may be particularly insidious in groups.

The French writer Michel Houellebecq, in his novel *Submission* (2015), defines submission as the greatest human desire:

"It's submission (…) The shocking and simple idea, which had never been so forcefully expressed, that the summit of human happiness resides in the most absolute submission." (p. 212)

In the novel, he imagines a possible France in the near future where all society, including the government and intellectuals, slowly submits to a kind of silent and "gentle" Islamic seizure of power, so that as women's rights disappear little by little, education becomes Islamic, yet everything happens without anyone rebelling. Yes, it is imagination, it is true, but it can occur in human societies. Faced with the advent of Nazism, in 1933 the psychoanalyst Willem Reich (author of an important book on character analysis) wonders not so much how the German people could accept it, but how they could *desire* it.

Because the projection of the Ego Ideal on the leader takes place within very tight libidinal bonds and with scarce critical sense, the leader can be a sadist or a pervert, as was the case in the Second World War and in other dictatorships. It can even be hypothesized that some civilizations disappeared due to the death drive, caused by their own dismantling.

Melancholy

Another important expression of the death drive which we find in both psychoanalytic and psychiatric clinics,[3] and also throughout the history of art and humanity, is melancholy. Freud calls melancholy the "pure culture of death drive" (1924).

Starting in 1923 with The Ego and the Id and a year later with his essay on masochism, the theory of the death drive is complete. It will become increasingly clear that for individual and collective life, Freud will have in mind the need for the drives to remain fused, or blended, and that the death drive, known as "destructive" from now on, is not untied from and does not lose its link with Eros in order not to kill the organism, if it is turned inwards as masochism, or the object if it is turned outwards as sadism. Melancholy is a significant example of unbinding, of the "pure culture of death drive." Having postulated the existence of an autonomous death drive in the organism, it obliges one part to be redirected externally as aggression so that the Ego is not overwhelmed, while a part will remain in the Ego as primary, or erogenous, masochism (1924). Before the theorization of the death drive, the unconscious mechanisms with which melancholy is formed, with which it is born, are described in the admirable essay *Mourning and Melancholia* (1915), but the concept of *fusion and defusion* had not yet been developed, the two forms in which, as we have seen, the two drives can exist – tied (fusion) or untied (defusion). With fusion, because the death drive remains mixed with Eros, life is not threatened; but with defusion, for some internal or external reason, this bond breaks and the death drive is now free to act and it affects the individual in its life thrust, in the desire for life, as we saw in the previous chapter in Spitz's neonatal marasmus.

Melancholy is a well-known condition in which a person completely loses the desire to live. Often, there is somatic involvement, such as sleep and appetite disorders (which for Freud and current psychiatry would suggest a constitutional genesis), suicidal thoughts, keening and anger, often only unconscious. It seems to resemble mourning but differs from it because in mourning (which normally lasts only a certain period), slowly the person returns to re-invest in themselves and the outside world, gradually abandoning the lost object, and life can resume. In mourning it is the world that is temporarily empty, not the Ego, as happens with melancholy (Freud, 1915). Moreover, in mourning the loss is conscious, you know what is lost, while in melancholy it is unconscious.

What makes the ego empty, devoid of libido, is the unbinding between the two drives: Eros is lost and so the person remains at the mercy of a "pure" death drive, that is, no longer bound and therefore free to destroy the Self.

From an economic point of view, there is a libidinal haemorrhage: The Ego, which had narcissistically invested its objects, when it loses them it finds itself emptied, as if the loss of object has become a loss of subject. The not infrequent flipping over to the opposite sentiment of mania according to Freud shows it is somatic origin, as if a person were born predisposed to suffer from melancholy.

We can map the predisposition to melancholy like this: we know that the melancholic is haunted by a particularly severe super-Ego, who blames them and makes them feel unworthy of everything, they are a bad person. The super-Ego is formed by unconscious identification with parental figures, and in general with the environment. This identification must be followed by an introjection, specific to each one, which preserves in part the characteristics of the parents and, above all, their super-Ego, which mixes with the specific characteristics of each one. This passage, which takes place at the end of the Oedipal stage and allows it to be overcome, involves a de-erotization and it is here that unbinding can take place.[4] Often, in fact, there is a family history of melancholy, and certainly a child in contact with a depressed mother does not receive the libidinal investment necessary for sufficient self-love, nor can they reflect in the maternal gaze which, in turn, is too depressed to recognize them. André Green spoke of the "complex of the dead mother" (1983) and Marie-Claude Lambotte wrote a very thorough essay on melancholy, beginning with the Freudian point of view of the death drive (1993). From an object relations point of view, the melancholic is someone who cannot repair their own love objects and is thus persecuted by guilt. But we have seen that, although clinically very similar, the death drive in the original Freudian spirit is not maintained here.

In any case, the melancholic lives internally in a climate of death, where everything is turned off: their vitality, their life drive, their investment in the outside world, which appears empty and dry. Not infrequently, these patients commit suicide, either directly or indirectly, through accidents, illnesses, or drug abuse.

It must also be said, however, that in psychism there are two faces to everything. In *Mourning and Melancholy* Freud raises the idea, without subsequent development, that perhaps melancholy allows access to the truth, so he writes of the melancholic: "He also seems to us justified in certain other self-accusations; it is merely that he *has a keener eye for the truth* than other people who are not melancholic" (1915, p. 246, my italics). This important detail, which Freud adds in this sibylline sentence, helps us to understand the possible link between art, thought, intuition, and melancholy.

Sara, the singer

Sara is 35 years old when she comes to ask for a second analysis; the first, to her satisfaction, helped her to move out of her parents' house to go and live on her own. She went into analysis after attempting suicide using drugs. She has always been depressed and melancholy. She thought she was feeling better then, during and immediately after

Covid-19, she feels as if she is falling back into depression, and so she comes to me. Sara is an artist, a singer and co-writer of her songs who has managed, through talent and will, to earn a living in a very competitive field.

She spends entire sessions or sometimes whole weeks (three sessions per week) crying, a subdued sobbing of true despair. Sara does not know why; as Freud wrote in *Mourning and Melancholia*, the melancholic does not know what they have lost, their loss is unconscious. Sometimes despair is stimulated by feeling rejected, or incapable, but they are not real triggers; hers is like a pain of existence. She is aware that depression, coupled with masochistic submission, has damaged her career. At the same time it is these experiences, when they can access poetic elaboration, that are the root of her inspiration.

During analysis Sara manages to feel better. The transference relationship already in itself "binds" the depressive anguish. The presence of the analyst – an attentive listener, punctual, participatory, never trivial – proves fundamental for a melancholic and creative patient, always at risk of being inundated with free death drive. The analytical relationship also remediates Sara's extremely strict sadistic super-Ego, which makes her feel stupid and worthless. The main object of analytical work with a melancholic patient should be the super-Ego, which slowly needs to be made friendlier and must be remediated so that it does not crush the Ego in a deadly grip. There is always a risk of unbinding and defusion, so Sara needs continuous work to maintain a strong bond with Eros and, consequently, with good internal objects.

Working with a creative melancholic is rather delicate. The analyst must tread a fine line in trying to soften the super-Ego and the Ideal of the Ego, both too strict, but leaving the patient an area of "good" sadness, of nostalgia and a yearning for a mythical lost object, because all this is also artistic nourishment.

Melancholy in artists and addiction

"Inspiration contained a death threat. He would, as he wrote the things he had waited and prayed for, fall apart. *Drink was a stabilizer*. It somewhat reduced the fatal intensity." (S. Bellow, *On John Cheever*, 1983, my italics)

So writes Saul Bellow about his ill-fated friend John Cheever, a great (and belatedly re-discovered) American writer who suffered from depression all his life, with which he coped through alcohol that caused his relatively early death. This is not an isolated incident.

Why are so many artists, men and women of genius, who have given so much to humanity through their work, so often self-destructive, and often end up committing suicide? I think of the poets Virginia Woolf and Sylvia Plath, a generation of great American writers, as well as Cheever, Ernest Hemingway, and F. Scott Fitzgerald or, more recently, David Foster Wallace, musicians such as Jimi Hendrix, Jim Morrison, or Kurt Cobain of Nirvana (a suggestive name for the death drive!), and many others, both in the past and today; to the melancholy of the poet Rainer Maria Rilke, to the suicide of the painter Mark Rothko in 1970, after many years of severe depression. I have only mentioned a handful contemporaries whose biographies are quite detailed, but the phenomenon has always existed. It cannot be denied that a genius, a great talent, often carries a germ of self-destructiveness, as we saw earlier with film director Lars von Trier.

Many hypotheses can be made, and the artistic phenomenon, as Freud also recognized, ultimately remains a mystery. But this is a book about the death drive, and we may hold it in account when trying to explain these phenomena, to which I will return in Chapter 8. Many of these artists committed suicide using drugs or alcohol, either directly or through the loosening of the defences that the substances cause which thus make suicide possible. This is the case with Fitzgerald and Hemingway, suicides after a long history of alcoholism and drugs.

So I have decided to consider depression in artists and drug addiction together, because they often go hand in hand, and I think addiction is a perfect paradigm of the death drive and, perhaps, the main contemporary psychopathology. In my view, the spectrum of addiction includes not only substances, but all behaviours in which the individual needs excitement to feel they exist or to confront their depressive demons. This excitement, however, can lead to short-lived euphoria, as was the case for David Foster Wallace during his creative stages, but it is euphoria that keeps the underlying depression at bay. Above all, I believe, in addictions of any kind (including food, gambling, etc.), the individual seeks, as Saul Bellow writes, *to reduce fatal intensity, to zero tension, to stillness,* to Nirvana, to reduce impulsive excess, to zero. Here, we are in the throes of the death drive.

Psychoanalytic studies on drug addiction are not as extensive as one would expect when compared with the huge spread of the phenomenon. I agree with Rik Loose (2000), when he observes that the literature of older psychoanalysis contained important contributions to the explanation of addiction through its relationship with libidinal developmental disorders, which post-Freudian scholars have since reductively underestimated. Freud, in *Civilization and its Discontents,* had recognized in *intoxication* one of the ways in which human beings have always tried to cope with the pain of living. He does not go beyond this bitter observation, where it seems implicit to be something that cannot be done without, because for most of us the pain of existence is inevitable. The first work entirely devoted to addiction is by the German psychoanalyst Karl Abraham (1908), who has much influence in early interpretations, where he argues that external influences and inheritance are not sufficient to explain these states, but there must be an individual, internal, factor tied to the libido. He senses that alcoholism could have to do with repressed homosexuality (present in every human being), which alcohol could uninhibit as well as uninhibiting exhibitionism and sadomasochism, which is why many violent crimes are committed under the influence of alcohol. Alcohol can become a substitute for sexual potency and represent a regressive tendency (in this sense note the link with perversions). "The drinker," he writes "makes use of alcohol as a means of obtaining pleasure without trouble" (1908, p. 88): in other words, what the Lacanians call, with regard to addiction, an enjoyment without the Other. Later, contributions by Edward Glover (1932) and Sandor Rado (1933), distance themselves from the pulsional aspects to address ego-psychology. Their thinking dominates the psychoanalytic interpretation of addiction for a long time. At first, even Rado (1926) remains faithful to the drive theory seeing an oral satisfaction in alcoholism. Later he sees it more as a search, by an Ego tormented by tensions and depressions, to find its primitive omnipotence, but this effect is only fleetingly obtained. In addition, all this happens under the punishment of the super-Ego. It is clear, therefore, that here Rado does not follow Freud on the theory of the death drive; for ego-psychology the death drive is a threat that comes from the *Es* (the Id), capable of destroying the integrity of the Ego, an aggressive and masochistic force that must be neutralized. The Ego fights against these deadly tendencies, but in the case of addiction, without success.

I believe the idea that the death drive should be countered by a strong Ego is erroneous and naive. As seen in Freud and Lacan, things are much more complex. We have seen, in Lacan, how life is not always something that wants to be nursed and looked after: life wants to enjoy. It is much more likely that in this lies the root of addiction, and because enjoyment also contains a mortal face, so often death (physical or psychic) is the outcome – not so much a weakness of the Ego, but rather its excess of impulse. The legacy of Rado's concept, still present today, tends to see addiction as a symptom, that is, according to the psychoanalytic definition of symptom, an often unsuccessful attempt to provide a solution to a conflict. This view is also not exempt from a certain moralistic halo, which sees the addict as a subject with no will. In my view it can be seen as a symptom, if we mean symptom as the container of pleasure or the beyond of pleasure, to which the subject is deeply attached. Glover (1928) broadens the view of addiction by seeing it as an escape from reality in fantasy, to satisfy sexual, oral and anal aspects of infancy, and to make it a pathology in its own right, a transition between neurosis and psychosis. Subsequently drawing nearer to Klein, he sees the effects of drugs as attempts to kill, punish or try to soothe introjected objects that disturb the subject, a self-medication to cure the suffering of the Self. In this sense, there is not much difference with the ego-psychology version. But his paper remains important for introducing the notion of a transitional state regarding addiction. In Kohut's psychoanalytic theory of Self Psychology, addiction is similarly a symptom of a fragile, infantile, non-cohesive and narcissistically vulnerable Self that struggles to regulate self-esteem.

For Lacanians, it is enjoyment without the Other (Cosenza, 2018), closed autistically in itself, which makes the subject avoid the passage of anguish,

> a marriage to drugs, an inanimate object that offers the addict unlimited enjoyment, hence in their libidinal economy it takes the place of the link with the phallus (desire) (…) to the uncertainty of the life of desire, conditioned by the otherness of the partner, in the new forms of the symptom the subject greatly prefers the certainty of the object of inanimate enjoyment.
>
> (ibid., p. 35, translated for this edition)

In short, we have, on the one hand, the vision of addiction as attempts to help a disturbed self through a sort of care of the self or, on the other hand, the vision of Lacan who, in addition to seeing an attempt at care of the self, adds to this the fundamental element of a pulsional enjoyment that goes beyond the limit. I agree with Loose (2000), author of an interesting review of the topic, that

> it is important not to articulate something at the level of the object (drug or alcohol), but to have something articulated at the level of

the subject. Only when operating with articulated signifiers will we perhaps learn something about the cause of addiction (...) If it is possible to consider addiction to be the waste-product – or (lost) object – of psychoanalysis, then psychoanalysis has to listen to how the object drug speaks in the subject. Only the spoken signifiers can determine the place of the drugs and their effect in the structure of the subject.

(p. 76)

There is no point in talking about the drugs object (to be fought), because it is, as with any pathology, a subjective experience that is articulated around the individual personality.

Let us look at an artistic example and a clinical vignette.

Excess as a death drive: The Whale by Darren Aronofsky (2022) and Mr. E.

Charlie is a respected university teacher. He gives online courses highly appreciated by students, but *he does not show himself.* On Zoom he keeps his camera off, nobody sees him. Charlie wants to hide his body, an obese body, of which he is ashamed. After deeply mourning his partner's death, which occurred after a stormy separation from his wife and estrangement from his daughter, Charlie "let himself go." By this guilt-ridden expression, one understands that it is about a person who has lost control of his drives, has given in to vice and excess, and will die as a result, as in Charlie's case. The director could have chosen a heroin addict, for example, more easily associated with addiction, but with great artistic talent (the film won several Oscars) he has instead chosen to personify obesity. This is a painful addiction that affects many people, who are not given the benefit of a traumatic history, unlike anorexia. Charlie starts to binge-eat after the bereavement: he doesn't want to think anymore, he doesn't want to remember anymore. He chooses to die by drowning in food, in the oral drive that is transformed, *in excess,* in what Lacan calls enjoyment, *jouissance*, the beyond pleasure, the heart of the death drive, the "most pulsional" *(triebhafter)*. In the film, the protagonist dies, but in many cases death is psychic, even if the person remains alive.

Mr. E. is a 30-year-old man, handsome but with an inexpressive face, who does not seem to possess a rich or articulated inner world. After having exhausted all the treatment options (including hospitalization, medication), pressed by his parents, he asks to see me. He is a gambler and an alcoholic. The two addictions go together: alcohol loosens his inhibitions. It makes Mr. E. feel calmer but more lively, able to be with others, and this allows him to go and play. He has lost two jobs, stolen his father's money and once ended up in jail for dealing drugs. Unfortunately, I only get to see this patient for a few months. After we established good contact and he was coming regularly to sessions three times a week, he stole from his parents and his father made him suspend his therapy and sent him to a rehab centre.

In the months when we saw each other, very significant elements had emerged. The youngest of four siblings, Mr. E. grew up feeling the least seen, the least brilliant, the one who disappointed the expectations of his father, a doctor, and so very early on he devoted himself to borderline behaviour, the use of soft drugs, until he discovered gambling and alcohol. In this manner he had found a way to feel valid, grandiose, worthy of attention from people, and spent evenings and nights "*like I'm on a merry-go-round... I no longer feel anything, nothing.*" A severe diabetic, he was aware that alcohol abuse put his life at serious risk. It was as if a small suicide occurred every night.

Like Charlie in *The Whale*, my hypothesis, with which the patient agreed, was that Mr. E. retreated into a world of excesses capable of both supplying him with a narcissistic return (when he gambled, he was admired by others, frequented cool clubs, had what he called "the good life") and with a turning off of, as he himself said, the negative emotions, and the very sense of living.

"*I feel alive only when I play, half-drunk ... after there is nothing.*"

It is also possible that stealing from his father, just when we were establishing a regular analysis, was a subconscious way of self-boycotting, of undermining a prospect of treatment that could have changed him.

In other cases, the very difficult challenge of treating patients with addiction has, in my experience, been more successful; cases in which the family is completely cooperative and can bear the relapses, in which a good relationship is established between analyst and patient where they feel understood and never judged, and there exists within them a part of Eros, even just a small one, which is trying to bear life.

In *Civilization and its Discontent* (1929), Freud points out that among the remedies that human beings try to control pain and endure life, one is precisely what they call "intoxication," that is, to dive into the easy world of addictions, which the contemporary market offers in super-abundance. Are we in an era at risk of death drive?

It is always hard to analyse the present, but it is something we should consider. I also believe that psychoanalysis, more prepared by these theories, which, as you can see, are far from abstract, could effectively address this vast swathe of patients, suffering from various types of addiction, generally considered as unsuitable for treatment. But that is not the case; besides patients like E., there are others for whom treatment is possible. I reference the case of N., a young patient about whom I wrote in another book on the death drive,[5] heavily addicted to alcohol, cocaine and marijuana, within a borderline-traits personality. By accepting analysis in four weekly sessions, after four years N. was able to almost stop the abuses entirely and to decide to be with a woman with whom he later had a child. A few years after we ended treatment, he returned for more analysis, which lasted about two years.

There is not enough space here to relate the whole treatment. Suffice to say that, as opposed to Mr. E., there was greater suffering in N., a sense of defeat and guilt, and consequently a desire for treatment. Perhaps in time this will also happen for Mr. E., if he remains alive. But in his case, the two addictions together formed an enjoyment. He derived from the oblivion deep satisfaction, something N. had lost.

I would also like to point out that in the transferal relationship with such patients, the analyst often feels useless, without meaning or motivation, as if they are working with someone *who is there by chance*, as if the patient did not care about himself or his mind, and delegated the analyst *to think for him, to try for him*. It is not an opposition or an attack, but a deficiency, as if the patient lacks a mind with which to think. The purpose of the death drive within addiction is exactly that, *to kill the mind*, to deaden thought, fantasy, desire as sources of unbearable tension.[6] The patient comes with his Nirvana, his desire only for peace. But the very fact of accepting treatment and coming to the session, even while remaining silent the whole time ("*You tell me*," said N. "*What do you want me to talk about?*") sometimes for long periods – that is as much as the patient can give.

The excess to be extinguished may concern artists, like many of our patients. People initially take drugs for pleasure; but after the 1920 breakthrough we see that pleasure always devolves into sorrow, *Lust* and *Unlust*.

Charlie, the protagonist of *The Whale* commits suicide with excess food to deal with grief and painful tension. Artists such as Fitzgerald, Van Gogh, Pollock, Foster Wallace and others throughout the ages are spent by drugs at the height of their success; more simply, in not infrequent cases such as Mr. E. and Patient N., they seek oblivion in drugs, depending on their temperament, the circumstances of their lives and the environment in which they grow up. Nothing like addiction is so close at hand.

"I have drunk since I was 15 and few things have given me more pleasure. When you work hard all day with your head and know you must work again the next day what else can change your ideas and make them run on a different plane like whisky? Modern life, too, is often a mechanical oppression and liquor is the only mechanical relief" (Hemingway 1935, Selected Letters p. 420, 1981).

Notes

1 Rudolph Bell's (1985) interesting research is noteworthy in *Holy anorexia,* a book about fasting and mysticism from the Middle Ages to the present day. He parallels modern anorexia with the extreme sacrifices and fasts of famous saints, such as Catherine of Siena and Clare of Assisi.
2 A 2020 film *The Blue Whale* by Egyptian director and actor Alaa Morsy was also made about the phenomenon and was streamed on Netflix in 2023.
3 In DSM-5 (APA, 2013) it corresponds to major depression (with or without manic episodes).
4 There are, of course, other readings of melancholy, which do not take into account the death drive, but there is general agreement on what is written in *Mourning and Melancholia*: the melancholic is someone who, in failing to detach from the lost object, interjects it but also retains inside the hatred and ambivalence they felt for it. The introjected object thus becomes a bad object that destroys the Ego, according to the famous Freudian phrase "the shadow of the object fell upon the ego" (Freud, 1917, p. 158). I also recommend Thomas Ogden's beautiful reading of *Mourning and Melancholia* (2007).
5 Valdrè R. (2019): *Psychoanalytic Reflections on the Freudian Death Drive in Theory, the Clinic and Art.* Routledge, London.
6 In Bionian terms one could speak of –K (attacks on thinking).

Chapter 6

The death drive and sublimation

A dangerous relationship

Let us return to the theory and to a previously raised question: why do self-destruction and often perversion lurk in so many artists, in genius? The French psychoanalyst Janine Chasseguet-Smirgel gives us a good explanation from a metapsychological point of view:

> The relationship between creation and perversion is *enigmatic*. Indeed, the creative process implies having resources to sublimation. Now, sublimation makes use of the same instinctual energy as which is directly released through perverse sexual activity. In both cases, it is pregenital libido. Pregenital instincts are the essential – and probably the sole – raw material for sublimation.
>
> (1984, p. 89)

Sublimation and perversion have *the same drive source*. They draw on the same initial mixture of partial drives and may take a more *objectivising* direction (Green, 1983), bound to objects and moving towards sublimation, or more *de-objectivising*, unbound and moving towards the death drive and perversion and, in the unbinding, perhaps mixing with melancholy, too. In humans, the highs and lows go together.

We must take a step back, still with Freud, and place the phenomenon of sublimation at the wellspring of art.

On sublimation

Paradoxically, a concept that has come into common use and of which everyone more or less knows its meaning, lacks a work that deals with it fully: there is no one specific Freudian essay on sublimation, so we

DOI: 10.4324/9781003474678-7

must trace it from several writings. Freud intended to devote one of the essays in *Metapsychology* (1915) to sublimation, but then did not. I agree with Green (1993) that Freud's great essay on sublimation is *Leonardo da Vinci and a Memory of his Childhood* (1910), even though all Freudian thought is interspersed with the concept.

The term is taken from chemistry and refers to the process by which a substance can change from one state to another (a solid into a gas, for example): it is a *transformation.*

In sublimation the sexual drive renounces the object of satisfaction and *shifts* to other, generally more abstract or cultural, goals that are equally capable of giving pleasure. Thought, art, in short, the whole of civilization, is based on sublimation, a concept for which Freud always had a high regard.

Clinically, we see it, for example, after an effective mourning, when the patient manages to abandon the lost object, such as a loved one, and move the libido to something *that represents them*, or when mourning becomes the opportunity to become creative in something never done before, or to implement changes, and so on. Freud writes:

> The sexual instinct (…) places extraordinarily large amounts of force at the disposal of civilized activity and it does this in virtue of its especially marked characteristic of being able to *displace its aim* without materially diminishing in intensity. This capacity to exchange its originally sexual aim for another one, which is no longer sexual but is psychically related to the first aim, is called the capacity for sublimation.
>
> (1908, p. 187)

Although intuitively simple, the process is complex. The erotic drive must change aim, renounce direct satisfaction (because it is no longer possible, for example) and find pleasure in a different way, through indirect, sublimated objects. Friendship, for example, is sublimated love, just as tenderness is a sublimated form of passion. We saw in the film *The Whale* that after deeply felt mourning the protagonist fails to disinvest the lost object and ends up dying in the excess.[1]

But can we all sublimate in the same way? And how is this process more powerful and more specific in artists?

Freud delves into this in his essay on Leonardo, the great genius who attracts his attention, as both artist and scientist. For Freud, da Vinci is a model of perfect sublimation, a rare specimen or, as Freud calls him, the "purest" one. When we reconstruct the artist's life and personality, we see that da Vinci had a very mild character. He did not love nor hate, having replaced love with a passion for knowledge, that is, an epistemophilic drive. Freud describes the great artist as someone who, from the beginning of his life, transformed childhood sexual curiosity into thirst for knowledge, preserving it from removal (ibid., 1910).[2] In most people, the process is not so pure, due to the removal of childhood desire, which can also lead to inhibition of knowledge, as well as sexuality (as is the case for David, my patient).

What is important to remember here is that sublimation is an unconscious process whose essential aspect is pulsational flexibility, which allows us to move the aim and replace a concrete object with a more abstract, symbolic one; in fact, sublimation and symbolization are closely linked, the two capacities go hand in hand (Klein, 1950; Segal, 1991).[3]

So, if we are talking about a psychic capacity with positive value, what does it have to do with the death drive and why did I entitle the chapter "a dangerous relationship"?

Sublimation and death drive: hypothesis

Some French psychoanalysts point out the possible contiguity between sublimation, when excessive, and the death drive. Green writes:

"The ego (…) promises heaven and lets go of the earthly love in which its life is rooted. By turning away from Eros, it has become the apologue of death" (1993, p. 226)

Because in order to detach itself from the object, sublimation always involves de-erotization, abandoning Eros can result in a dangerous proximity to the death drive, as is the case with any libidinal detachment. An example may be extreme asceticism, in which the drive body is totally erased, or severe anorexia, where analytical treatment is almost impossible because they have cancelled any libidinal relationship, as with the "anorexic saints" described by Bell (1985) and mentioned in the previous chapter. The sexual drive is offered a great *chance:* to transform, to become something else, to detach itself from the direct object of pleasure and invest in its representation, that is, to renounce the object but maintain its internal representation (Valdrè, 2014). This passage involves risks when it is undertaken too rigorously. In line with Freud, I believe that sublimation is maintained in the territory of Eros. It is the main aid to human life to access symbols and thought, and *only* in particular situations (which at this point means sublimation is no longer the correct term) such as asceticism, anorexia, certain forms of autism, does it cross over into death.

However, because it is still an "eagle with two heads," (David, 1998) in the clinic a close watch must be kept with certain patients and the excesses of erotic disinvestment, the excesses of deprivation that can untie the deadly drive. Freud cautions about this when he writes to the Swiss Lutheran minister and lay psychoanalyst Pastor Pfister:

> But you are in the fortunate position of being able to lead them to God (…). For us this way of disposing of the matter does not exist (…) and, as the other ways of sublimation which we substitute for religion are too difficult for most patients, our treatment generally results in the seeking out of satisfaction.
>
> (1909)

Pushing too hard to sublimate those who are not capable, he adds, can cause harm and the patient will find himself worse off than when he arrived. Had he been able to sublimate, he would not have fallen ill. The clinician must be attentive and sensitive to the sublimatory abilities of each patient, because some are unable to give up direct investment. I would summarize this brief note on this aspect of possible contiguity, by using Green's words:

> Sublimation-desexualisation would be an adverse pulsation to sexuality (…) On the one hand sublimation appears a vicissitude of the sexual drive, a purified form which has its place among other possible destinies, but which remains in the patrimony of Eros and, on the other, sublimation is the adverse counterpart of Eros which, far from serving its aims, sides with those forces which are antagonistic to its purpose. The paradox cannot easily be overcome (…).
>
> (1999, p. 219)

Because as we have seen sublimation is more pronounced in artists, contiguity with the death drive is, too. This explains the coexistence of great capabilities and terrifying collapses in many artists.

In her diaries, the sculptor Louise Bourgeois tries to describe this struggle between life and death that inhabits her, and that she always tries to dominate through her work. She writes,

> I am an addictive type of person and the only way to stop the addiction is to become addicted to something else, something less harmful. What the substitute is is the body of my work. The sculptures

reveal a whole life based on eroticism; *the sexual or the absence of sex is everything.*

(1998, pp. 227–228, italics my own)

Usefulness of the death drive

There is another aspect in which the whole complexity of the death drive and its intricate relationship with the life drive is highlighted, what has been called the subjectivation function (Le Guen, 1989; Penot, 2017). What does that mean?

We have seen that staying alive depends on the mixture of the two drives, life and death, not on the prevalence of one. One cannot live with the life drive alone. The usefulness – indeed, the *necessity* – of the death drive must be recognized. The unbinding work is deadly only when it is completely detached from Eros, but a certain amount of unbinding, of disinvestment, is needed to encourage new investments: mourning, sublimating, detaching from the primary object to invest in the third (father), dissolving mass identifications in groups resulting from excess of Eros. The title of Bernard Penot's article published in the *International Journal of Psychoanalysis* in 2017 is quite clear, *The so-called death drive, an indispensable force for any subjective life* (pp. 299–321). To become autonomous subjects, it is necessary to detach oneself; after all, life is a collection of bereavements, of detachments. All of these detachments, from the mother onwards, in metapsychological terms depend on the ability to unbind the drive; otherwise, the individual remains stuck to the first object or, adhesively, to the groups.

An important clinical-historical observation in this regard is that of the French psychoanalyst Nathalie Zaltzman[4]: psychic functions can be more clearly framed in extreme circumstances. Zaltzman (1998) defines the death drive as "anarchic:" in particular, extreme conditions for survival, this drive can represent a vitalistic, rebellious current that can help to save the human being.

"I call this version of the death drive, the most individualistic, the most libertarian, the anarchist drive" (Zaltzman, 1998, p. 139, translated for this edition).

She posits that in extreme situations, such as in a concentration camp, some subjects are able to mobilize equally extreme drive forces, of death, yes, but paradoxically protective, which can help them face the deadly challenges. All of us, when we are in danger or face great obstacles engage in real "libidinal struggles" to stay alive, as with serious trauma and accidents.

I remember the case of Mrs. S., a woman in her forties who was in deep depression over her husband's abandonment. She revitalized when she was able to engage in the child-custody proceedings that followed. Without developing persecutory feelings, she had an unexpected awakening of life. There was a purpose to remain alive, permanently detaching herself from her husband.

From other points of view, one could read Zaltzman's reflections as "restorative" instances, such as the existence within us of good internal objects to resist in these situations; admittedly, theoretical approaches are not mutually exclusive (i.e., more strictly Freudian or a more object relations approach), but I believe that at certain times the life-death drive dialectic is ignited, and some people, strong or even heroic ones in particular, manage better than others to "disinvest to live." Perhaps it corresponds to what is now called resilience.

Thus, far from considering the death drive (understood as the ability to unbind) as the main factor of subjectivation, its contribution is fundamental. The French psychoanalyst Claude Le Guen (1989) speaks of centripetal and centrifugal forces in human development: the former bind, invest in the object; the latter flee and unbind. Bond excess would result in the subject's collapse onto the object, as in certain psychoses in which there has never been detachment from the primary object and Lacanian *jouissance* occurs. Other authors, such as Winnicott (1971), speak of "non-integration" to indicate a concept analogous to unbinding, that is, a state of disorder to be periodically experienced in order to be subjective. After all, it is the difficult task of the individual to become an autonomous subject. This task, incomplete or never ending for some, lasts for a lifetime, and is always threatened by centripetal, regressive forces that would like to turn back.

Narcissism should not be overlooked in the role in which the death drive is placed at the service of the Ego. As Green (2010) elaborates, the life drive stands in defence of the Ego through narcissism, which prevents us from destroying ourselves. In Green's revisitation, narcissism is the cement, the glue that holds together the life drive and the bond with the object. When this bond is lost and the world becomes devoid of objects (unobjectal) death prevails.

Going back to the clinic, the pathologies in which this de-objectivizing unbinding brings about a deadly scenario, are today represented by the whole spectrum of addictions, états-limites[5] and traditional melancholies as well.

If we have seen that the death drive has a positive aspect, we can assume that this is also the case for its derivatives. In fact, there exists a masochism that I have called necessary (Valdrè, 2020) and Rosenberg (1991) calls "guardian of life."

"Necessary" masochism

I define necessary masochism as the normal masochism of daily life and of life in general.

The initial metapsychological observation is due to Benno Rosenberg, a French author who deepens and even radicalizes Freud's thought on masochism, and distinguishes the two "faces" of masochism, namely deadly masochism and "guardian of life" (1991).[6] His argument is complex, but we can summarize it starting from the observation of one of the three types of masochism seen by Freud (1924), primary masochism or erogenous masochism that we saw as being that part of the original death drive *linked to Eros*, not projected outwards but libidinally tied to ensure a primigenial vital nucleus. In his careful examination, Rosenberg notes that in the passage between the pleasure principle and the principle of reality (referencing Freud's *Formulations on the Two Principles of Mental Functioning* of 1911) a capacity to bear the displeasure has to take over. "In other words," he writes, "it is because the pleasure principle encompasses masochistic pleasure, implies the possibility of *pleasure in displeasure,* which can be transformed into the principle of reality" (Rosenberg, 1991, p. 65, translated for this edition, italics my own).

The pleasure principle, that is, must be tempered, we cannot live inundated with pleasure, and in this toning down masochism comes into play. The term masochism is perhaps associated with its most serious and pathological forms, but we must think of all those behaviours, however small or large, in our lives that involve enduring a quota of displeasure: making a sacrifice for someone, giving birth ("basic" masochism, for Green, 1983), renouncing, delaying a desire. On the other hand, deadly masochism is "a masochism that has succeeded too well. This means that the subject masochistically invests all suffering, all pain, all or almost all the territory of displeasure" (Rosenberg, 1991, p. 84, translated for this edition). This form of masochism, because of its abandonment of the tie with the object, is also called deadly autism (ibid., p. 85), and essentially does not protect against destructivity. In the clinic we see it in self-mutilation, severe anorexia and non-delusional psychoses.

In essence, the death drive and masochism endanger life when they are excessive and unbound from Eros, but when they are bound to Eros they protect, allow development and enable us to endure life and its travails.

Notes

1　Excess in this case means the excess of food.
2　I delve deeply into sublimation in all its aspects in *On Sublimation: A Path to the Destiny of Desire, Theory and Treatment* (Karnac, 2014).
3　Although Kleinian authors speak of repair rather than sublimation, both processes lead to symbolization and in this sense are analogous. Repair, however, has to do with the object, while sublimation with the drive and the goal.
4　She was an original figure in French psychoanalysis who, with Piera Aulagnier, was part of the so-called Quatrième Groupe.
5　I prefer, for these cases, to use the état-limite concept coined by Green (1990), rather than borderline. Although both are very close to self-destruction, in a borderline the link with the object is more maintained, hence the well-known symptoms of anger and explosiveness when it is felt to be absent or insufficient, while in an état-limite emptiness prevails, it is an object desert and also, clinically, anger may not be present. I refer, for this type of borderline structure, mainly to Kernberg's concepts (1976).
6　Unfortunately, there is still no English translation of *Masochisme mortifère et masochisme gardien de la vie* (Rosenberg, 1991). For an illustration of his thought in English, see Penot (2022): *Reflections on Masochism: An Introduction*, IJP.

Chapter 7

The reason for a fundamental concept on human nature

I have tried to illustrate in the previous chapters why the death drive should not be relegated to something abstract and metaphysical, as it is continuously reified in human life, both individual as well as group and social.

We have seen how this is a Freudian concept, developed above all by French psychoanalysis, but clinically accepted, at least partially, by some contemporary post-Kleinians. We have also seen the elements considered critical.

We have highlighted the importance of its life-threatening derivatives, such as masochism and melancholy, but also its subtle expression in addiction and some personality disorders, such as état limite, that are now widespread.

We have also seen, however, how the death drive is paradoxically necessary in order to live because its unbinding from objects allows the person to grow, to be subjectivized.

What is important to remember is that this great Freudian metaphor, born from the need to understand the complexity of human nature that does not obey the pleasure principle alone, as was thought until 1920, serves to explain the multiform aspects of behaviours that are not easily explained: masochism, pleasure in pain, the search for Nirvana, self-harm. I agree with Green when he writes:

No one wants to listen to anyone talking about the death drive, but everything that is put there to replace it to have a clearer conception sends us back to the death drive. And there are some attempts at reformulations to overcome the reformulation presented by Freud (…) But that does not change the problem; the problem is

DOI: 10.4324/9781003474678-8

that there is destructiveness admitted by these authors, that hinders analytic work.

(in Urribarri, 2013, pp. 125–126)

Understanding the death drive, in fact, helps us to better understand, as Green writes in this passage, resistances to analytical work that are not explainable, such as a negative therapeutic reaction and some types of repetition compulsion. Nonetheless, it is not a simple matter because we have also seen all the ambiguity and complexity of the relationship between the life drive and the death drive. To reiterate, *both* are necessary, but life is allowed only as long as they remain *bound* (what Freud calls *fusion*), if instead they *unbind (defusion)*, the pleasure principle that drives people to live is cancelled. It is a very fine line then.

One of the most frequent disguises of the death drive is aggression. Aggression in a healthy person is most often at the service of the life drive. It is expressed in the sexual act, which requires a certain quota of sadism. It is the emotional thrust to defend vital interests (or life itself) in the face of deadly threats.

Perhaps, lastly, the main expression of the death drive is death: do you need a drive to die? The question is both intriguing and disturbing, but because a drive exists in order to live, the organism must also equip itself with its counterbalance. As the American cultural critic Lynne Tillman writes in the beautiful *Mothercare: On Obligation, Love, Death, and Ambivalence* (2022):

Dying is an activity, the organs go about their task toward entropy; needing time to shut down. The body is active to the end. It is so odd. Without eating and drinking, people can live up to two weeks.

(p. 116)

This passage, not written by a psychoanalyst, makes us understand how, regardless of whether one agrees with Freud's thesis, his courage in investigating death *in psychoanalytic terms* should be acknowledged. He did not take it for granted, as an inevitable external event. Only Freud, in my opinion, with the death drive, places death itself *in the organism*, being already part of human baggage from the beginning.

What usually triggers the death drive? I believe that this question relates to the other, also controversial, issue of what may be at the root of old age and death. Proponents of an endogenous theory speak of a biological clock based on genetics and/or phylo-genetically transmitted from our ancestors. Everyone has "their own time," already programmed from birth, in which they must age and die. Others, more likely to consider exogenous factors, believe that senescence and death depend on the accumulation of the harmful effect produced by external agents of different kinds, such as toxic, infectious, emotional, relational, cultural, or social factors. From this perspective, in the absence of such factors we would theoretically be immortal! I believe that isolating the features of each of these two theories (endogenous and exogenous) is arbitrary: each feature is always closely interconnected with all the features, and is produced or activated, strengthened or weakened, by them. Biological fragility, on a genetic or acquired basis, a failure of interpersonal relationships, social pressures, and cultural factors, most often come into operation concomitantly, and the death drive no longer meets sufficient resistance.

Perhaps one "chooses" to die when the impulse of life is exhausted; as Freud writes, "the organism wishes to die only in its own fashion" (1920, p. 39). Understanding that there is a death drive can help us as psychoanalysts to not always feel responsible for therapeutic failures, but equally to consider that sometimes, with certain patients, one does everything possible, and it is still a success to keep them alive, Green writes at the end of his work (Green, 2010).

This is a fundamental concept, even when it is not shared.

The presence of a death drive helps us to understand the nature of phenomena such as certain types of repetition compulsion, repetition of the identical in which the patient always brings back the same painful and dysfunctional experiences onto the scene, but does not detach from them.[1]

Of course, pathological identifications and cumulative trauma also come into play in these cases (Khan, 1963), but in my opinion this does not exclude the drive basis of these behaviours. It helps us to understand everything that happens *beyond* the pleasure principle and the complexity of human pleasure.

As we will see in the next chapter, it also helps us to understand the phenomena of psychic inertia, which are also a major obstacle to therapy. Humans do not want to change, it would seem. We aspire to stillness, to stasis. As Lacan writes, man dreams of dying (1959–1960) and the Ego, as Green writes, wants nothing more than to be left alone (1990). This makes psychoanalysis an impossible profession;

at journey's end, Freud acknowledges this in *Analysis Terminable and Interminable* (1937): the resistances to change in most people are insuperable.

Inertia: Mark's case

Mark prepared his report for the congress with great care. It would result in his formal entry into the academic community he had just joined and, above all, allow him to make known his work and his thought. Mark is a PhD student in economics. This is his chance. He prepared himself meticulously, but when the day comes for him to deliver his report, something in him isn't working. The night before, he had a few extra beers in his hotel to calm down. Now he is tired and can't wait to leave. Not to actually leave, he will tell me when he returns, but "*at some point, all I thought about was going back to my room, relaxing, binge watching a series, drinking and sleeping... how I wanted to sleep!*" The sleep to which Mark aspires is an escape from enormous tension, facing an audience, having to speak; his whole body and being are in revolt.

Years of study and fatigue now seem to be frustrated by the *desire to sleep*, to "*stay in the hotel alone... empty the minibar, watch TV... no one looking for me.*"

Freud writes that:

> We cannot fail to recognise that the satisfaction of the instinct is accompanied by an extraordinarily *high degree of narcissistic enjoyment*, owing to its presenting the ego with a fulfilment of the latter's old wishes for omnipotence.
>
> (1930, p. 121)

Here, in 1929 while writing *Civilization and its Discontents*, Freud expands his conceptualization, linking the death drive and narcissism, the search for a sort of fusion with, we can now add, an archaic omnipotent object, a breast that eternally nourishes without asking. Mark's congress ends in failure, but on his return to the analysis room this was not readily interpretable. First Mark had to recognize *within himself* the reasons for this intolerance of desire, this masochistic research of Nirvana. The only child of parents of modest means who sacrificed to get him through his education, Mark grew up with the heavy burden of "*having to recompense, living up to expectations ... always in debt.*"

I do not have the space here to report Mark's story in full, but it can be said that certainly, on that day at the congress, chasing Nirvana television, indulging the push to inertia instead of action, Mark finally realizes a composite unconscious desire: to disobey the internal parents, regain his peace, punish himself for the success he achieved. His father was plunged into a financial meltdown in his youth. Mark grew up sensing, without really understanding, a great sorrow in his father, for which he should have made up for by becoming successful. So, in this complex drift during the congress, Mark also put in place a repetition.

How can we *not* repeat, ask Ansermet and Magistretti (2010), how can we forgo a painful/pleasant dependence on an unconscious phantom from which we cannot detach?

> When all the conditions are met for an expected pleasure, suddenly we are no longer interested. And sometimes the object of desire, once attained, does not bring the expected pleasure, probably because pleasure was, at the end of the day, more in the desire than in the object: there is pleasure in desiring.
>
> (Ansermet, Magistretti, 2010, p. 7, translated for this edition)

Pleasure is no longer a compass, Ansermet and Magistretti say, it is not what orients us. There is a misunderstanding in pleasure. Things take place on two different levels: we have a conscious, rational, sequential logic that respects contradictions and deals with oppositions; and we also have an unconscious, adimensional logic, governed directly by the immediate needs of pleasure and responding to the primary process, which, as we know, is characterized by the absence of contradiction and negation, and is atemporal and aspatial. The question of pleasure may, therefore, prove to be ambiguous and somewhat enigmatic. The psychoanalyst Ansermet and neurobiologist Magistretti, both Swiss, have been collaborating for years on studies on pleasure, free energy and, therefore, the death drive, as we will see in the next chapter. I think that, for a clinician, it is necessary to question the contradictory nature of pleasure in human beings, who are guided by drives, not instincts, indeed, are flooded by a continuous drive excess that they must govern. With the theorization of the death drive, while not necessarily considering it entirely accurate, Freud nevertheless provides us with fundamental keys to understand, or attempting to understand, this mysterious world that afflicts us and our patients, this world of ours which is *beyond pleasure*.

Note

1 Here I refer to some types of repetition compulsion because sometimes in repetition there can be the unconscious desire to elaborate and transform, as we see in analysis. I appreciate Michel de M'Uzan's subtle distinction between repetition of the same and repetition of the identical (*le même et l'identique*), where only the identical is on the side of the death drive (1969).

Chapter 8

Future developments
The contribution of neuroscience

I would like to start by saying that even though it was Freud's wish, I do not think it is necessary for psychoanalytic theories to be scientifically proven. For reasons of completeness, however, I will close this book with the interesting perspectives on the death drive that have unfolded in recent years thanks to neuroscience. Certainly, death drive is inserted within drive theory, and an understanding of its general structure is therefore necessary, as described by Freud in his *Project for a Scientific Psychology.* The essay dates back to 1895, but Freud's doubts about the energy theories contained in it prevented him from publishing it, so *Project for a Scientific Psychology* came to print only in 1950. Seventy-plus years later, it has become a source of interest for neuroscientific studies. I have tried to group together what is interesting about contemporary research in two main strands, one finding in favour of his intuition, the other finding against.

Finding in favour: the "Franco-Swiss" strand

An early interesting study confirming the Freudian intuition contained in *Beyond the Pleasure Principle,* emerged in the late 1990s, in immunologist Jean Claude Ameisen's (1999) book *La sculpture du vivant.* In it, he reports that without a shadow of a doubt human cells face the paradoxical phenomenon of cellular suicide, also called apoptosis. Each human cell contains, from conception, the possibility of suicide if it does not find a suitable environment for survival – it has the ability to self-destruct in a few hours (Ameisen, 1999, p. 13). The phenomenon of apoptosis has long been known (Kir and Miller, cited in Doninotti, 2011) as cellular implosion, but Ameisen describes it more fully as a process where the cell triggers its suicide by detaching itself from the

DOI: 10.4324/9781003474678-9

nearby cells, fragmenting itself until the exit of enzymes that destroy the surrounding environment, a death that predicts neither lesions, nor scars, nor inflammation, and the surrounding cells fill the void left by the dead cells (ibid., p. 122). We are *sculpted*, as Ameisen says in the title, from birth into death, as if life were not a foregone process, but something that happens *despite* the possibility of continuous cellular death. This work resonates strongly with the Freudian assertion that "if we are to take it as a truth that knows no exception that everything living dies for internal reasons – becomes inorganic once again – then we shall be compelled to say that *the aim of all life is death*" (Freud, 1920, p. 38). In general, neuroscience confirms the need for harmony, for homeostasis to which the body tends. The seat of the circuits that guarantee the homeostaticity of the impulses has been identified in the mesencephalic region of the insula, imaginatively named by Ansermet (2010) as "l'île de la pulsion," or drive island. That is the area of the brain that tells us if we are cold to take shelter, if we are hungry to eat. The insula, in its anterior region, would also govern the *somatic representation* of a drive, for example faced with the hunger stimulus, the designated neuronal group represents ahead of time the pleasure connected to food. At the level of the anterior and posterior insula there is *discontinuity* in play. The dynamic movement at this level seems to be at the basis of homeostasis (the *principle of constancy* mentioned by Freud in *Project for a Scientific Psychology*). According to these researchers, a part of the insula, which they call S, presides over somatic states derived directly from the sense organs, and another part, called R, presides over the representation of these somatic states. When we are *overwhelmed* by a trauma,[1] in dementia, in psychosomatic diseases, in the life of the infant, the S system invades, exceeds R and representation is not possible. We can hypothesize how much of the pathology that comes into our analysis rooms, such as panic attacks or "generalised anxiety," fits into this pattern, in which the somatic excess of impulse goes beyond the capacity for representation, that is, of thought, dream, symbol. What is necessary for the capacity to represent to be established at the beginning in the newborn infant is the intervention of the other, of the maternal object that modulates this excess impulse. Laplanche speaks of *translation* of the enigmatic message (2016), Bion of capacity for revery (1962), in general of mirroring and a reflective function (Winnicott, 1965; Fonagy, 1997).

Another theory, that of opposing processes (Ansermet, 2010), describes the existence of a dopaminergic system which presides over the discharge (pleasure), to which another system would be opposed, especially as time passes. This is the basis of the tolerance observed in all addictions and makes them over time capable of causing unbearable pain or even of becoming fatal. These authors postulate that there is also a similar process underlying repetition compulsion, namely a dependence on a mechanism that initially brings pleasure, but then exhausts that capacity and causes displeasure, but is repeated anyway. As Ansermet writes:

> Life is not a pleasure ride. When everything is in place for life to go smoothly, for access to pleasure to be possible, that is when we contrive to trap ourselves, against our will, to achieve displeasure. Worse still: sometimes we even repeat what leads to displeasure, as if we were seized by a pleasure in the displeasure.
>
> (Ansermet, 2010, p. 199, translated for this edition)

It is important to point out that, from this perspective, the theory expressed in *Beyond the Pleasure Principle* would not be a change of direction in Freud, but a continuation of that principle of constancy, or inertia, already expressed in 1895 in *Project for a Scientific Psychology*, considered a *precursor of the death drive* (Tran The et al., 2020). Hence,

> certain aporias that seem inherent to the concept of the death drive can be overcome if we consider them in the context of an epistemological model that draws on the paradigms of physics which were conveyed by the Helmholtz School.[2] Namely, we can consider the death drive in reference to the principle on entropy and the laws of thermodynamics.
>
> (ibid., 2020, p. 1)

Hence the work from which this strand of neuroscientific studies begins dates back to early Freud, to 1895, when he postulates that the first principle concerning the nerve cell is to arrive at "zero tension," that is, the principle of neuronal inertia. Neurons try to reach or restore zero excitement quantities (Q), according to a principle of inertia defined as "neurones tend to divest themselves of Q" (Freud, 1895, p. 296).

In accordance with Ameisen's theory seen earlier, according to these researchers, life would self-destruct, compensated at all times by a process of creation. The death drive is therefore only apparently a new concept in Freud in 1920, deriving instead consistently, throughout his thought, from the principle of inertia of 1895. A straight and coherent line links the studies of 1895, with the principle of inertia, and the essay of 1920 with the death drive. This is not a question of scientific aberrations, but a theory of the living being that arises within late 19th-century epistemology, of which Freud is an heir.

Finding against: the neuro-hormonal approach

More critical authors, on the other hand, consider the issue to be much more complex. The pleasure principle leads to endorphin secretion. Research shows that such a mechanism is activated in gambling and other addictions, but only if preceded by *chronic frustration* (Kirsch et al., 2022). The impulse element, according to this other strand of study, would not be sufficient without the intervention of the frustrating environment. Returning to Mark's case, it is as if it were said here that his inertial addiction behaviour (and masochism) would have been possible because it was preceded by traumatic situations or cumulative micro-traumas (such as his father's work problems, unconscious identification with a losing figure, etc.). In contemporary psychoanalysis we always return to the diatribe between drive and object theory: does the subject prevail, with their unconscious drive world, regulated by physical and biological laws, or does the environment prevail, with its ability to satisfy or frustrate? I do not believe that, on a subject as complex as the human mind, the two approaches must necessarily be in conflict; nor do I believe that Freud had in mind the model of an isolated mind, a kind of monad, as certainly as the father of psychoanalysis, he was concerned to construct a sufficiently scientific model of the psychic apparatus. We have evidence that as early as the *Project for a Scientific Psychology* he already introduces the notion of the object when he speaks of the "experience of satisfaction" – a reaction to the filling (*Erfüllung*, which also means "fulfillment") of the neurone by a pressure or urgency that results in a motor discharge. He specifies that, *being incapable of feeding itself*, the infant succeeds in this way in calling up *"extraneous help"* (p. 318) – or in other words an adult, who satisfies the need for nourishment and subsequently becomes a "memory of the object" whose image may, should the need arise once again, be hallucinated (p. 319).

Moreover, in unleashing psychic pathological events, Freud has always recognized the so-called but little-mentioned complemental series (Freud, 1938): personal drives and the role of the environment *complement each other*, never acting on one another alone.

These more critical researchers have also investigated the other aspect of Freud's biological roots, primary or erogenous masochism. It has been seen that in pleasure experiences (sexual, for example, or in addiction), beta-endorphins (also known as feel-good hormones) are released. These endorphins also govern pain because pain relief has been shown to produce pleasure (Watanabe and Narita, 2018); so it is entirely possible that the masochist uses *pain relief* to accelerate pleasure, in orgasm, for instance (Henry, 1982). This is, in my view, the biochemical understanding of "libidinal co-excitation" (Freud, 1924), due to which painful stimulation is generally capable of causing even a certain excitement. The idea of a primary masochism in the human being is therefore confirmed, but it is more activable when there are also traumas or insecure attachment models, so that:

> A death drive can be established when a psychological trauma has corrupted essential drives, especially attachment, so that physiological release of beta-endorphins is limited.
>
> (Kirsch et al., 2022)

In the same work though we also read that a pathological release of endorphins is possible to compensate for the deficit that the trauma has caused. What can we infer from this? The most damaged patient will be the one who, to compensate for the endorphin deficiency that traumas have caused them, will use pain, *pain relief,* to obtain pleasure, to ease the pain (psychic and physical) by triggering the release of endorphins. All this is amply confirmed by our daily clinical experience: those who have been damaged unconsciously seek trauma, they seek new *damaged bonds* (Eigen, 2001), as if trapped in a tragic paradox. We see it in the tenacity of certain negative transferences, in negative therapeutic reactions and in the observation of life in general. An abused or ill-treated child can easily become an adult who either becomes an abuser themself (by identification with the aggressor) or submits to the same situations experienced in childhood (think of Mrs. B., abused as a child, as well as neglected by her mother, she ends up marrying a sadistic and perverse man).

The same repetitive pattern is applicable in addiction and was observed by this same research group in gambling disorder (ibid.). According to this view, hormones would be the physiological correlation of the drives, substances that are released or inhibited in the experiences of pleasure and displeasure. Hunger, thirst, sleep, sex, primary needs of attachment are conveyed by the release of beta-endorphins. They confer pleasure. In healthy people a certain endorphin level in the brain tends to be established, which may become euphoria if release increases. It has been observed that in masochism and gambling disorder, the two disorders taken as examples in this study, the same occurs, namely a large endorphin release, and therefore an intense pleasure which would, however, compensate for a primary hormonal regulation deficit (in psychoanalytic language, "drive" would replace "hormonal").

> For most people under regular circumstances, sexual masochist activities or gambling in an amusement hall are nothing more than latent alternative options that will not be automatically activated when the essential drives are optimally satisfied. They only become active in a repetitive manner once the essential drives are persistently corrupted and become disorders when this frustration is chronic.
>
> (Kirsch et al., 2022, p. 8)

Death drives would be triggered when there is a trigger for unmet primary needs, when a traumatic root already exists. Perhaps when Mr. E. described the pleasure of the game as "*like I'm on a merry-go-round*," he was describing this endorphin invasion.[3]

Clearly, in both of these strands, the researchers themselves say that further research is needed, given the complexity of the human brain, the labyrinth of neural networks, neurotransmitters and hormones that act in extremely complex interweavings.

As a conclusion, albeit provisional and limited for the moment, of everything I have tried to summarize, my position follows that of Freud's "complemental series." Why should the two approaches necessarily be mutually exclusive? I am inclined, as the Swiss say, to consider the death drive described in *Beyond the Pleasure Principle* of 1920 as an evolution of the 1895 principle of inertia, or rather, an idea that Freud never abandoned about the functioning of the psychic apparatus, but which becomes a death drive only after clinical observations and social developments that, at the turn of 1920, make it clearer *how* this principle of inertia can be expressed. I believe that we must distinguish the "true" death drive, to be understood as this continuation of the principle of inertia,[4] which leads a human being to tend to erase tensions and anxieties linked to life, to the life drive, whose clinical and social expressions can be observed in various phenomena: addiction pathologies, Nirvana, some repetition compulsion and childhood games, passivity in groups and masses, some psychosomatic diseases, masochism, and, finally, death itself.

This death drive, properly Freudian, must be distinguished from forms of aggression, violence, and destructiveness as understood by Kleinian and post-Kleinian authors and partly by Kernberg, which can represent *active* expressions *of* the death drive projected outwards, on objects, to get rid of it. We see it active in different psychopathologies, such as those described by Kernberg (1976), and in severe borderline disorders and narcissists, during some moments of analytical work with these patients and on a social level in wars. Freud has always believed that aggression, in order to express itself, also needs a little Eros; it aims at the death of the object, of the other, as a first need.

Given this distinction, the neuroscientific approaches previously set out do not necessarily seem to be mutually exclusive. Or rather, there is something in the psychic apparatus that we can call the death drive, and consider it exclusively innate or, as is more likely, accentuated by initial traumatic experiences that lead the psyche to call up painful circuits, in the paradoxical intent of soothing the initial damage.

Notes

1 Here I mean trauma in the Freudian sense, as an excess of stimuli (internal or external) that invade the protective shield against stimuli to the point where they cannot be blocked. Today, a protective shield against stimuli is regarded as a biological concept which appears in mental life as the striving to avoid unpleasant affects. Trauma is a twofold concept in that it relates to mental experience and links an external event with the specific after-effects on an individual's psychic reality. Central to this is the concept of excess in relation to how much an individual can protect himself. It follows that trauma is especially crucial in childhood.

2 Of the German neurophysiologists by whom Freud was influenced, Helmholtz was undoubtedly the most important (Jones, 1953). This school aimed to link the principles of thermodynamics to human functioning.

3 As seen in studies conducted on casino players, Mr. E. also *played to lose*. Some players, even if they win, continue to play until they lose, thus revealing the masochistic nature behind the game (Bergler, 1957).

4 I use the principle of constancy or inertia indistinctly because I consider the two terms to overlap. Although Swiss researchers sometimes make a distinction, I do not think it is necessary.

Conclusions

It is not easy to draw a conclusive profile of this intriguing concept, this deadly inertial thrust of the psychic apparatus that Freud called the death drive and that in the end is a term we all continue to use. What we can certainly agree on is that this concept possesses an extraordinary fertility, not only in clinical and theoretical terms but in the whole field of human thought. Few other concepts in psychoanalysis have caused such a stir, and perhaps none has constituted a breakthrough, such as the so-called watershed of 1920, which changed psychoanalytic theory and the way we conceive humankind.

In any case, at the heart of the death drive concept is the fundamental Freudian discovery that a *beyond the pleasure principle* exists, a shocking discovery that blows a hole in every optimistic or naive vision of progress and development. The human being, whether as an individual or a group, does not necessarily tend towards the good, neither their own individual good nor the good of the community. Unlike any other living being, the human being remains *faithful to the trauma*; and so, as we have seen from several psychoanalytic and neuroscientific points of view, for there to be development, this quota of deadly drive cannot find too much of a free field (it is *bound, tied*) nor can it encounter on its path, especially at the beginning, an excess of trauma or chronic and cumulative traumas (which would leave the drive *unbound, free*).

Kulturarbeit (Freud, 1929), the work of civilization, understood in the Freudian sense of *Kultur*, is capable of *binding* the destructive drive above everything else, and extends to every human action operating

DOI: 10.4324/9781003474678-10

through thought and culture. But this work is always threatened by deadly impulses:

> In short, the closer the state of fusion is, the more the death drives are bound by the life drives, and the more unbinding is neutralized. It is illusory to hope for a total suppression of the effects of the death drive; the ambivalence one always discovers, which never disappears completely, is proof that they will never be completely suppressed.
>
> (Green, 2010, p. 68)

Like Penelope who at night unravels the garment she has woven during the day, so the two drive types work – making and unmaking, tying and untying – for as long as there is life. We must not, therefore, as is the case in certain psychoanalytic orientations, reduce the concept of the death drive to aggression or violence, for it tells us much more about human nature. It also puts the *relationship with time* into play.

Green (2010) writes that repetition compulsion is the "murder of time." The death drive would like this, a still, motionless time that does not pass, that always returns. Although Freud rarely speaks explicitly of *nostalgia,* there seems to be something nostalgic when he describes the death drive. But what kind of nostalgia? The return to the inorganic, to the quietness of the "before life," seems to indicate an ontological nostalgia on behalf of the human being, not for what has been lost, but rather for what has never been had. The nostalgia of a perennial quietness, which some may identify with the "breast" or an "oceanic feeling" (Freud, 1929), recounted so beautifully by poets and writers.

Of course, the murder of time, because it hates any progress, can reify itself as aggression, and then the patient does not want to heal, does not want to change and prefers unconsciously to cocoon in repetitions, or to seek balm in addiction. But aggression, in the Freudian sense, is only secondary, just a projection necessary for the primitive death drive and the primitive masochism that inhabit us. In fact, in his 1924 essay *The Economic Problem of Masochism*, Freud, contrary to what he had postulated in *Three Essays on the Theory of Sexuality* in 1905, states that it is masochism that is primary and sadism that is secondary. Some psychoanalysts, such as the Kleinians, do not share this approach and consider sadism as the primary; but in the Freudian vision, which is necessarily prevalent in this book and in my own vision, because the concept we have dealt with is a Freudian concept, the need to attack the object is only secondary to the need to expel out of the self a quota of the death drive. This implies, as Freud recalls in his bitter remarks in his correspondence with Einstein (1932), that we will never be free from destructiveness, if it is a necessary projection of the death drive, that we will cyclically have to wage wars and destroy each other if it is necessary to manage and project an excess impulse of innate death.

Beyond the Pleasure Principle is not a work that makes concessions. The vision of human nature it offers us is disturbing. It is one of an individual inhabited, from birth, by impulses that work against their growth, impulses that desire death, which is understood above all as the death of desire. Hence Lacan, with his usual provocation, says that "life dreams of dying" (1959–1960).

We have seen in this short book the various theoretical, clinical, social, artistic and neuroscientific aspects of this troubling concept. We have seen that the death drive is silent and therefore even more insidious. Clinically speaking, we must find it in certain *impasses* in analysis, in tenacious resistance, in drugs of all kinds, in repetition, because we all know how to recognize external aggression, but what is difficult is the recognition of *internal* aggression, and even more so if this procures paradoxical enjoyment.

Having listed in the previous chapters all the aspects that seem to me to have to do with the death drive, I would like to conclude here with what, as I said, is perhaps the heart of Freudian reflection: a drive within us that wants to kill time. So analytical and therapeutic work in general is truly impossible! But so is psychoanalysis as, in accordance with the view of time that French psychoanalyst Jean-Bertrand Pontalis expresses in his fine book *Ce temps qui ne passe pas* (1997),[1] we believe that psychoanalysis, if it wishes to remain alive, cannot be of its time – that is to say, conforming to its own time, but always of "another time or an other time," relatively indifferent to common sense, fashions and prevailing thought.

Precisely because of its relative indifference to common time, perhaps only psychoanalysis can deal with the death drive. Because it *exceeds* time in the chronological sense, through its tools – setting, free associations, transference – psychoanalysis occupies *another* time, the time of repetition. Transference is repetition, but in treatment it becomes a running engine that can make progress, or not, and it can lend itself to the service of defence.

When the patient I talked about in the first chapter, Mrs. G., refers to her neglectful lover by saying "*I do not know what I regret*," she is bringing into analysis her personal killing of time: in the blurred shadow of her lover, she tries to find a father who, always so far away for work, on his return relieved her from maternal depression. Today, at 62, Mrs. G. is an educated and intelligent woman, yet she seems to be stuck in childhood. The person she brings to analysis is *also* that little girl who was waiting for her father so as not to sink into depression. Hence the analyst can, instead of feeling attacked by this resistance, return together with the patient to the time of that child, a time that nostalgically and utterly in vain she tries to reproduce with every man she meets. Not only in direct transfer, but also in the numerous lateral transfers that a patient makes in life, can we perceive repetition and the death drive.

Therefore, to those who adduce or complain of a crisis in psychoanalysis, I would say that this crisis does not exist if, indeed, psychoanalysis manages to remain "untimely" in the sense of Nietzsche's *Untimely Meditations*,[2] that is to say, able to sustain the magical balance of *including oneself inside while keeping oneself outside*.

Of course, having theorized a death drive should not discourage us from continuing our work, but it cautions us against easy enthusiasm. With this theory, which Freud offers us, clinicians must know that they are dealing with a force, both within themselves as well as within the patient, some in particular, that is rowing in the opposite direction – that pain and passivity are not necessarily something avoided in order to protect oneself but can also constitute an end and something sought after, even tenaciously. If we tune into these counterintuitive, profound and paradoxical aspects of human nature, aware that we also have them in ourselves, then analytical work, so complex and almost impossible, becomes, like art, among the most authentic of human experiences.

Notes

1 Pontalis' book has not been translated into English.
2 A collection of Nietzsche's essays on German culture published between 1873 and 1876, untranslatably entitled *Unzeitgemässe Betrachtungen*, which have been published in English under varying titles, including *Untimely Meditations* and *Unmodern Observations*.

Bibliography

Abraham K. (1908): *The Psychological Relation between Sexuality and Alcoholism*. Selected Papers on Psychoanalysis. London: Karnac, 1988

Akhtar S. (2017): The tripod of terrorism. *International Forum of Psychoanalysis*, 26: 139–159

Ameisen J.C. (1999): *La sculpture du vivant. Le suicide cellulaire ou la mort créatrice*. Paris: Éditions du Seuil

Ansermet S., Magistretti P. (2010): *Les Énigmes du plaisir*. Paris: Les Éditions Odile Jacob

Assoun P.-L. (1993): *Freud et les sciences sociales*. Paris: Armand Colin

Assoun P.-L. (2007): *Leçons psychanalytiques sur le masochisme*. Paris: Anthropos

Bell D. (2015): The death drive: Phenomenological perspectives in contemporary Kleinian theory. *The International Journal of Psychoanalysis*, 96: 411–423

Bell R. (1985): *Holy Anorexia*. Chicago: University of Chicago Press

Bellow S. (1983): *On John Cheever*. Retrieved from www.nybooks.com/articles/1983/02/17/on-john-cheever

Benvenuto S. (2003): Freud and Masochism. *Journal of European Psychoanalysis*, 16: Winter-Spring 2003

Bergler E. (1957): *The Psychology of Gambling*. New York: Hill and Wang

Bion W.R. (1959): Attacks on linking. *International Journal of Psychoanalysis*, 40: 308–315

Bion W.R. (1965): *Transformations*. London: Karnac, 2002

Bolognini S. (1994): Transference: Erotised, erotic, loving, affectionate. *The International Journal of Psychoanalysis*, 75: 73–86

Bolognini S. (2008): *New Reflections on Narcissism*. Paper presented at the Psychoanalytic Centre of Milan

Bourgeois L. (1998): *Destruction of the Father/Reconstruction of the Father*. Writings and Interviews (1923-1997). London: Violette Editions

Brenner C. (1959): The masochistic character: Genesis and treatment. *Journal of the American Psychoanalytic Association*, 7(2): 197–226

Chasseguet-Smirgel J. (1985): *Creativity and Perversion*. London: Free Association Books

Collins R. (2008): *Violence: A Micro-sociological Theory*. Princeton: Princeton University Press

Cooper A. (1988): *Masochism: Current Psychoanalytic Perspectives*. New York: The Analytic Press

Cosenza D. (2018): *Il Cibo e L'inconscio. Psicoanalisi e Disturbi Alimentari*. Milan: Franco Angeli

Couvreur C. (1989): Une équation à deux inconnues. *Revue Française de Psychanalyse*, 53: 643–660

David C. (1998): Un aigle à deux têtes: sublimer mais à quelle fin? *Revue Française de Psychanalyse*, 4: 1109–1122

Deleuze G. (1967): *Présentation de Sacher-Masoch. Avec le texte intégral de La Venus à la fourrure*. Paris: Les Éditions de Minuit

Deleuze G. (1971): *Masochism: Coldness and Cruelty*. New York: Zone Books, 1991

De M'Uzan M. (1999): Le même et l'identique. *Revue Française de Psychanalyse*, 34: 442–453

Deutsch H. (1945): *The Psychology of Women*. New York: Grune & Stratton

Deutsch H. (1965): *Neuroses and Character Types*. New York: International Universities Press

Doninotti E. (2011): *Psicoanalisi della distruttività. La pulsione di morte*. Padua, Italy: Upsel Domeneghini Editore

Eigen M. (2001): *Damaged Bonds*. London: Karnac

Fenichel O. (1935): A Critique of the Death Instinct. *The Collected Papers of Otto Fenichel* (First Series). Vol. 1. New York: W. W. Norton, 1953

Fenichel O. (1945): *The Psychoanalytic Theory of Neurosis*. London: Routledge, 1996

Ferenczi S. (1929): The unwelcome child and his death instinct. *The International Journal of Psychoanalysis*, 10: 125–129

Ferenczi S. (1930–1932): Notes and fragments. *The International Journal of Psychoanalysis*, 30: 231–242

Ferenczi S. (1995): *The Clinical Diary of Sándor Ferenczi*. Cambridge, MA: Harvard University Press

Feldman M. (2000): Some views of the manifestation of the death instincts in clinical work. *The International Journal of Psychoanalysis*, 81: 53–65

Fonagy P. (1997): Attachment and reflective function: their role in self-organization. *Development and Psychopathology*, 9: 679–700

Fiumanò M. (2016): *Masochismi Ordinari*. Milano: Mimesis

Freud A. (1936): *The Ego and the Mechanisms of Defence*. London: Karnac, 1993

Freud S. (1895): *Project for a Scientific Psychology*, S.E. 1. London: Hogarth

Freud S. (1905): *Three Essays on the Theory of Sexuality*, S.E. 7. London: Hogarth

Freud S. (1908): *'Civilized' Sexual Morality and Modern Nervous Illness*, S.E. 9. London: Hogarth

Freud S. (1910): *Leonardo da Vinci and a Memory of his Childhood*, S.E. 11 (pp. 59–137). London: Hogarth

Freud S. (1911): *Formulations on the Two Principles of Mental Functioning*, S.E. 12. London: Hogarth

Freud S. (1915a): *Thoughts for the Times on War and Death*, S.E. 14. London: Hogarth

Freud S. (1915b): *Instincts and Their Vicissitudes*, S.E. 14. London: Hogarth

Freud S. (1915c): *Mourning and Melancholia*, S.E.14. London: Hogarth

Freud S. (1916). *Some Character-Types Met with in Psycho-Analytic Work*, S.E. 14: 310–333. London: Hogarth

Freud S. (1919a): *A Child is Being Beaten*, S.E. 18. London: Hogarth

Freud S. (1919b): *The Uncanny*, S.E. 18. London: Hogarth

Freud S. (1920): *Beyond the Pleasure Principle*, S.E. 18. London: Hogarth

Freud S. (1921): *Group Psychology and the Analysis of the Ego*, S.E. 18. London: Hogarth

Freud S. (1923): *The Ego and the Id*, S.E. 19. London: Hogarth

Freud S. (1924): *The Economic Problem of Masochism*, S.E. 19. London: Hogarth

Freud S. (1926): *Inhibitions, Symptoms and Anxiety*, S.E. 21. London: Hogarth

Freud S. (1927): *Dostoevsky and the Parricide*, S.E. 21. London: Hogarth

Freud S. (1929): *Civilization and its Discontents*, S.E. 21. London: Hogarth

Freud S. (1932): *Why War? Letter to Einstein*, S.E. 22. London: Hogarth

Freud S. (1937): *Analysis Terminable and Interminable*, S.E. 23. London: Hogarth

Freud S. (1938): *An Outline of Psycho-Analysis and Other Works*, S.E. 23. London: Hogarth

Gay P. (1988): *Freud: A Life for Our Time*. London: J.M. Dent & Sons

Glover E. (1932): *On the Etiology of Drug-Addiction. On the Early Development of Mind*. London: Imago Publishing, 81–90

Glover E. (1928): *The Etiology of Alcoholism. On the Early Development of Mind*. London: Imago Publishing

Green A. (1983): *Life Narcissism, Death Narcissism*. A. Weller (Trans.). London: Free Association Books, 2001

Green A. (1990): *La Folie privée (On Private Madness)*. London: Karnac, 1996

Green A. (1993): *Le Travail du négatif (The Work of the Negative)*. New York: Free Association Books, 1999

Green A. (2010): *Illusions and Disillusions of Psychoanalytic Work*. London: Karnac

Hemingway E. (1981): *Selected Letters* 1917–1961. C. Baker (Ed.). New York: Scribner Classics

Henry J.L. (1982): Circulating opioids: Possible physiological work in nervous central functions. *Neuroscience & Biobehavioral Reviews*, 6: 229–235

Houellebecq M. (2015): *Submission*. New York: Farrar, Straus and Giroux

Jones E. (1953): *The Life and Work of Sigmund Freud, V1: The Formative Years and the Great Discoveries, 1856-1900*. New York: Basic Books

Joseph B. (1982): Addiction to near-death. *The International Journal of Psychoanalysis*, 63: 449–456

Kernberg O. (1976): *Object-Relations Theory and Clinical Psychoanalysis*. New York: Jason Aronson

Kernberg O. (1988): *Clinical Dimension of Masochism. Masochism: Current Psychoanalytical Perspectives*. New York: The Analytic Press

Kernberg O. (2009): The concept of the death drive. A clinical perspective. *The International Journal of Psychoanalysis*, 90: 1009–1023

Khan M.M.R. (1963): The concept of cumulative trauma. *The Psychoanalytic Study of the Child*, 18: 286–306

Kirsch M., Dimitrijevic A., Buchholz M.B. (2022): "Death Drive" Scientifically reconsidered: Not a drive but a collection of trauma-induced auto-addictive diseases. *Frontiers in Psychology*, 13: 941328

Klein M. (1936): *Weaning. On the Bringing Up of Children*. London: Kegan Paul

Klein M. (1950): *Contributions to Pyschoanalysis*. London: Hogarth

Klein M. (1957): *Envy and Gratitude. A Study of Unconscious Forces*. London: Routledge

Kohut H. (1971): *The Analysis of the Self: A Systematic Approach to the Psychoanalytic Treatment of Narcissistic Personality Disorder*. New York: International Universities Press

Kohut H. (1977): *The Restoration of the Self*. New York: International Universities Press

Krafft-Ebing R. (1886): *Psychopathia Sexualis*. Stuttgart, Germany: Enke

Kristeva J. (2005): L'impudence d'énoncer: la langue maternelle. *Revue Française de Psychanalyse*, 69: 1655–1667

Kundera M. (1984): *The Unbearable Lightness of Being*. New York: Harper & Row

Lacan J. (1953): *The Function and Field of Speech and Language in Psychoanalysis. Ecrits: A Selection*. A. Sheridan (Trans.) 30–113. London: Tavistock, 1977

Lacan J. (1954): *The Seminar. Book II. The Ego in Freud's Theory and in the Technique of Psychoanalysis, 1954–1955*. New York: W. W. Norton, 1988

Lacan J. (1959–1960): *The Seminar. Book VII. The Ethics of Psychoanalysis*. London: Routledge, 1992

Lacan J. (1962–1963): *The Seminar. Book X. Anxiety*. New York: Polity Press, 2014

Lacan J. (1964): *The Seminar. Book XI. The Four Fundamental Concepts of Psychoanalysis*. A. Sheridan (Trans.). New York: W. W. Norton, 1977

Lacan J. (1958): *Guiding Remarks for a Congress on Feminine Sexuality. Écrits*, B. Fink, (trans.) London/New York, Norton, 2006, p. 615.

Lambotte M.-C. (2000): Figure mélancolique du masochisme. *L'énigme du masochisme*. Paris: PUF

Laplanche J. (1991): *Elementi per una metapsicologia*. Rome: Borla

Laplanche J. (2000): *Masochisme et sexualité. L'énigme du masochisme*. Paris: PUF

Laplanche J. (2008): *Sublimation. Problematique III*. Paris: PUF

Laplanche J. (1970): *Vie et mort en psychanalyse*. Paris: Flammarion

Laplanche J. (1987): *Nouveaux fondements pour la psychanalyse*. Paris: PUF

Le Guen C. (1989): Du bon usage de la pulsion de mort. *Revue Française de Psychanalyse*, 53: 535–554

Loose R. (2000): The addicted subject caught between the ego and the drive: the post-Freudian reduction and simplification of a complex clinical problem. *Psychoanalytische Perspectieven*, 2000(No. 41/42): 55–81

McWilliams N. (1994): *Psychoanalytic Diagnosis: Understanding Personality Structure in the Clinical Process*. New York: Guilford Press

Odgen T. (2007): A new reading of the origins of object relations theory. *On Freud's Mourning and Melancholia* (Ed. Bokanowski T.). London: Routledge

Penot B. (2006): Ladite " pulsion de mort ", une force indispensable à la vie subjective. *Revue Française de Psychanalyse*, 70: 767–780

Penot B. (2017): The so-called death drive, an indispensable force for any subjective life. *The International Journal of Psychoanalysis*, 98: 299–321

Rado S. (1926): The psychic effects of intoxicants: An attempt to evolve a psycho-analytical theory of morbid cravings. *The International Journal of Psychoanalysis*, 12: 396–341

Rado S. (1933): The psychoanalysis of pharmacothymia (drug addiction). *Journal of Substance Abuse Treatment*, 1: 59–68

Reich W. (1933). *The Mass Psychology of Fascism*. New York: Aakar Books, 2018

Reik T. (1941): *Masochism in Modern Man*. New York: Grove Press

Rivière J. (1929): *Womanliness as a Masquerade. The Inner World and Joan Riviere – Collected Papers 1920-1958*. London: Karnac 1991

Rosenberg B. (1991): *Masochisme mortifère et masochisme gardien de la vie*. Paris: PUF

Rosenfeld H. (1975): *The Negative Therapeutic Reaction*. Vol 2. New York: Jason Aronson

Roussillon R. (2000): Paradoxes et pluralité de la pulsion de mort: l'identité de perception. *L'invention de la pulsion de mort* (Ed. Guillaumin J.) Paris: Dunod

Sartre J.-P. (1943): L'être et le néant. *(Being and Nothingness)*. Hazel (Trans), Barnes (Ed.). New York: Washington Square Press, 1984

Segal H. (1973): *Introduction to the Work of Melanie Klein*. London: Karnac

Segal H. (1991): *Dream, Phantasy and Art*. London: Karnac

Segal H. (1993). On the clinical usefulness of the concept of death instinct. *The International Journal of Psychoanalysis*, 74: 55–61

Solms M. (2021): Revision of drive theory. *Journal of the American Psychoanalytic Association*, 69: 1033–1091

Spielrein S. (1912): Deconstruction as a cause of coming into being. *Journal of Analytical Psychology*, 39: 155–156, 1994

Spitz R. (1945): Hospitalism: An inquiry into the genesis of psychic conditions in early childhood. *The Psychoanalytic Study of the Child*, 15: 53–74

Steiner J. (1993): *Psychic Retreats: Pathological Organizations in Psychotic, Neurotic and Borderline Patients*. London: Routledge

Stolorow R.D. (1975): The narcissist function of masochism (and Sadism). *The International Journal of Psychoanalysis*, 56: 441–448

Tillman L. (2022): *Mothercare: On Obligation, Love, Death, and Ambivalence*. New York: Soft Skull Press

Tran The et al. (2020): From the principle of inertia to the death drive: The influence of the second law of thermodynamics on the Freudian theory of the psychical apparatus. *Frontiers in Psychology*, 11: Article 325

Urribarri F. (2013): An interview with André Green: On a psychoanalytic journey from 1960 to 2011. *The Greening of Psychoanalysis: André Green's New Paradigm in Contemporary Theories and Practice* (Ed. Kohon G., Perelberg R.). London: Karnac

Watanabe M., Narita M. (2018): Brain reward circuit and pain. *Advances in Pain Research: Mechanisms and Modulation of Chronic Pain* (Ed. Shyru B.C., Tominaga M.) Vol. 1099: 201–210. Singapore: Springer

Winnicott D. (1965): *The Maturational Processes and the Facilitating Environment: Studies in the Theory of Emotional Development*. London: Routledge, 1990

Winnicott D. (1967): *Mirror-Role of Mother and Family in Child Development. The Collected Works of D. W. Winnicott: Volume 8, 1967-1968*. Oxford: Oxford University Press, 2016

Winnicott D. (1971): *Playing and Reality*. London: Routledge, 2005

Valdrè R. (2014): *On Sublimation: A Path to the Destiny of Desire, Theory, and Treatment*. London: Karnac

Valdrè R. (2019): *Psychoanalytic Reflections on the Freudian Death Drive in Theory, the Clinic and Art*. London: Routledge

Valdrè R. (2020): *Sul masochismo. L'enigma della psicoanalisi. Riflessioni nella teoria, nella clinica, nell'arte*. Turin: Celad

Zaltzman N. (1998): *La pulsion anarchiste. De la guérison psychanalytique*. Paris: PUF

Filmography

The Whale. (2022) Darren Aronofsky
The Blue Whale. (2020) Alaa Morsy
Venus in Fur. (2013) Roman Polanski
Breaking the Waves. (1996) Lars von Trier

Index

Note: Page numbers followed by "n" denote endnotes.

Le Guen, C. 26, 70
Leonardo da Vinci and a Memory of his Childhood (Freud) 66
Lévi-Strauss, C. 31
libidinal bond 53, 54
libidinal co-excitation 36, 52, 83
libidinal developmental disorders 58–59
libidinal haemorrhage 55
libidinal struggles 69–70
libido drives 12, 19, 26, 41, 48, 55, 59, 66
life *vs.* death narcissism 25, 26
linguistics 18–20
Loose, R. 58, 60
Low, B. 16n12

Magistretti, P. 77
mask of suicide 52
masochism 54; beyond of pleasure 2; in cinema 50–52; definition 34–36; economic problem 38–42; feminine, problem of 37, 44–46; Freudian path 36–38; gambling disorder 84; importance of 3; life-threatening derivatives 73; melancholy 54–55; mysterious 3, 38; and narcissism 46–49; necessary 71–72; open book 43–44; primary/erogenous 83; primitive 88; psychopathology of trauma 38; self-punishment 42–43; success 42; types 39–41
masochistic perversion 34, 35, 40, 46, 47
mass psychology 53–54
maternal depression 90
melancholia: artists and addiction 57–64; definition 54–56; masochism 73; repetition and psychopathologies 3
Melancholia (Freud) 50
Meltzer, D.A. 28, 29
memory of the object 82
mental retardation 46
Metapsychology (Freud) 66
minimum necessary narcissism 46

Mitchell, S. 29
moral masochism 35, 40–41
Morrison, J. 58
Moses and Monotheism (Freud) 11
Mothercare: On Obligation, Love, Death, and Ambivalence (Tillman) 74
Mourning and Melancholia (Freud) 17, 55–57, 64n4

narcissism 70; and aggression 29; destructive 25–26; life *vs.* death 25, 26; masochism and 46–49
The Narcissistic Function of Masochism (and Sadism) (Stolorow) 47
narcissistic integrity 47
necessary masochism 71–72
negative and white psychosis 25
negative therapeutic reactions 2–3, 5, 40, 74
neural networks 84
neuro-hormonal approach 82–85
neuronal system 6
neurosis 60
neurotransmitters 84
Nietzschean eternal recurrence theory 9
Nietzsche, F. 8, 9, 90
Nirvana principle 1, 12, 18, 20, 30, 58, 63, 73, 76, 77, 85
non-delusional psychoses 71
non-genital sexuality 33n2
non-integration 70
nostalgia 32, 57, 88

objectivising 25, 26, 65
Ogden, T. 64n4
On Narcissism (Freud) 11
On Those Wrecked By Success (Freud) 42, 50

pain relief 83
panic attacks 80
passivity 10, 36, 37, 45, 46, 90
Penot, B. 26, 69
personality disorders 30, 73